SPIRIT AND *Life*

A collection of in-depth bible studies

Taught and Written by

DALE HEIL

Copyright © 2022 Dale Heil.

All rights reserved. No part of this book may be reproduced, stored, or transmitted by any means—whether auditory, graphic, mechanical, or electronic—without written permission of both publisher and author, except in the case of brief excerpts used in critical articles and reviews. Unauthorized reproduction of any part of this work is illegal and is punishable by law.

Unless otherwise indicated, scripture quotations are taken from The King James Version (KJV). Copyright © 1967, 1998 by Oxford University Press, Inc.; The King James Study Bible. Copyright © 2001 by G.E.M. Publishing; The Names of God Bible (NOG). Copyright © 2011 by Baker Publishing Group; and The Amplified Bible. Copyright © 1987 by The Zondervan Corporation and the Lockman Foundation.

ISBN: 979-8-88640-088-5 (sc)
ISBN: 979-8-88640-089-2 (hc)
ISBN: 979-8-88640-090-8 (e)

Because of the dynamic nature of the Internet, any web addresses or links contained in this book may have changed since publication and may no longer be valid. The views expressed in this work are solely those of the author and do not necessarily reflect the views of the publisher, and the publisher hereby disclaims any responsibility for them.

One Galleria Blvd., Suite 1900, Metairie, LA 70001
1-888-421-2397

CONTENTS

Foreword v
Introduction vii

Chapter 1 Biblical Salvation 1
Chapter 2 Like Father Like Son (Or Daughter) 15
Chapter 3 A New Beginning 21
Chapter 4 What's in Your House 24
Chapter 5 Putting God First 28
Chapter 6 Exercise Thyself Unto Godliness 34
Chapter 7 True Commitment 40
Chapter 8 Steadfast 46
Chapter 9 Seeking God 51
Chapter 10 Faithfulness 61
Chapter 11 Separation 65
Chapter 12 The People's Choice 80
Chapter 13 Repairing the Breaches in Our Lives 87
Chapter 14 Be Careful What You Eat 92
Chapter 15 Be Careful What You Speak 101
Chapter 16 Knowing God's Will 109
Chapter 17 According to Your Faith be it Unto You 113
Chapter 18 Abiding in Christ 121
Chapter 19 Strangers and Pilgrims 125
Chapter 20 Going Through (WaTer and Fire) 130
Chapter 21 Afflictions, Persecutions, Trials and Tribulations 135

Chapter 22 God's Mighty Men 145
Chapter 23 Our Spiritual Warfare 149
Chapter 24 Be Strong and of Good Courage 153
Chapter 25 Fighting for Our Deliverances 158
Chapter 26 The Land of Giants 162
Chapter 27 More Are They That Are With Us Than They
            That Are Against Us 167
Chapter 28 To the Victor Belongs the Spoil 174
Chapter 29 Taking Away the High Places 180
Chapter 30 Obedience is Better than Sacrifice 184
Chapter 31 The Danger of Compromise 190
Chapter 32 The Results of Sin in a Believers Life 196
Chapter 33 The Sin of Pride 203
Chapter 34 A Humble Spirit 208
Chapter 35 The Double Minded 213
Chapter 36 The Seriousness of Sexual Sin 216
Chapter 37 God's Enabling Grace 221
Chapter 38 An Expected End 225

About the Author 233

FOREWORD

Dale Heil is a man who has been diligent to present himself approved, to God a worker who rightly divides the word of truth. An amazing teacher, an inspiring speaker who will through this book bring a clearer understanding of Gods word, and will for our lives, to the reader. You'll find this book a real blessing and will be glad you read it.

Michael Peirce
Greeley, CO
July 2014

I have been greatly impressed by the dedication and fervor that Mr. Heil has submitted himself into the research for his writing. As a close brother who is compassionate in the Lord, his efforts are shown in words and deeds.

One should dare not miss out on receiving the insights shared.

Brother and friend, Roger J Matthews
Denver, CO
July 2014

As I edited and read each chapter of Dale's book I received the revelation of how the veil covers the scriptures. In 2 Corinthians 3:15 it tells us "Yet, even today, when they read the books of Moses, a veil covers their minds". (NOG) As you open this book prayerfully ask the Father to reveal his son Jesus through the scriptures to you and open your mind to see Him. In Corinthians 3:16 it says "whenever a person turns to the Lord, the veil is taken away". (NOG) In Mark 8:17 Jesus did ask his disciples if their minds was closed? Ask Him to open your mind to His word. Luke 24:45 says, "Then he opened their minds to understand the Scriptures". (NOG) This book will reveal the deep revelation of Jesus Christ from the book of Genesis to the book of Revelation. I pray as you read these chapters you will come into a personal relationship with Jesus in a whole new level that will bring everything to life in you that the Father has created you to be. When Jesus was on the cross, according to Matthew 27:51, the curtain or veil was split in two from top to bottom. That same resurrection power is for us today. He said He is life itself in John 11:25 and if we believe in Him we will not die. Jesus also said he is the bread of life. In Luke 24:35 the two disciples recognized Jesus when he broke the bread with them. Take communion with the Lord before you read this book and believe you will recognize Jesus in a new way.

Marilyn Anderson Meeker, CO
July 2014

INTRODUCTION

This book contains an assortment of in-depth bible studies on many different topics. The knowledge and insight from over twenty years of diligently searching the scriptures has gone into each of these messages. These studies made such an impact to save, change and reform so many lives as they were being taught, I felt lead to share them with as many as possible. These studies had a powerful effect on prisoners in the Colorado Correctional Facilities, and dramatically changed and reformed many of their lives. Many are now faithful members to churches outside of the prison walls and live productive godly lives.

This book can be read from beginning to end as the studies taught are arranged to bring a person to salvation, and then promote godly living and spiritual growth. However, as each chapter is on a different topic they can also be read in any order that one chooses. Each study goes beyond the surface teaching of God's Word to reveal in-depth spiritual truths. They are written simple enough to show the way of salvation to the unsaved, to feed newborn babes in Christ with milk, and are in-depth enough to feed the most mature Christian with the meat of God's Word. No matter where a person is in their Christian walk this book can be a great aid to spiritual maturity. All can greatly benefit from it. Many of these studies examine the poor spiritual condition and worldliness of individuals and the church as a whole, and what the bible instructs us to do that will bring correction. At the very least each one of us can examine our own life and the condition of our walk with God.

I have been advised not to speak on the poor spiritual condition of the church, or speak against the world if I am to be a popular Christian author. However that would make me to be one of the many teaching what the people want to hear (2 Tim. 4:2-4). It is better to reach a few that truly desire to live holy before God than the multitudes that look for excuses continuing to live in carnality. By picking up this book shows the hunger you have to live a holy life for God.

I pray that this book will greatly bless and enrich the lives of all that read it.

Chapter 1

BIBLICAL SALVATION

S alvation is a subject that many take far too lightly. Many seem to take salvation for granted, relying solely on having said the sinner's prayer at some point, but without really knowing what it is to have a true salvation experience. Saying the sinner's prayer most likely originated from the scripture reference in Romans 10:9-10, which states:

> **That if thou shalt confess with thy mouth the Lord Jesus, and shalt believe in thine heart that God hath raised him from the dead, thou shalt be saved. For with the heart man believeth unto righteousness; and with the mouth confession is made unto salvation.**

Although this is essential for salvation, one cannot base their salvation on just this one scripture, but must take all of God's Word into consideration. For instance, this scripture says that if a person shall confess with their mouth the Lord Jesus, and shalt believe in their heart that God has raised Him from the dead, that person shall be saved. However, there are countless people who have made this confession with their mouth who have never received salvation. Jesus Himself stated:

> **Not every one that saith unto me Lord, Lord, shall enter into the kingdom of heaven; but he that doeth the will of my father which is in heaven. Many will say to me in that day, Lord, Lord, have we not prophesied in thy name? and in thy name have cast out devils? And in thy name done many wonderful works? And then will I profess unto them, I never knew you: depart from me, ye that work iniquity** (Matt. 7:21-23).

Therefore, MANY who think or believe that they have received salvation have not. There are many who live a religious life, doing what they believe is service to Christ, but will not enter into the kingdom of God. Religion does not save anyone. Many view Christianity as a religion, which requires the outward keeping of laws, duties, and rituals as a means for salvation. That is not true Christianity. True Christianity is to be born of God's Spirit (Jn. 3:1-8, Acts 2:1-4, 10:44-48), by which we receive His divine nature (2 Pet. 1:3-4). The result is a life progressively lived by nature according to the things contained in God's law, showing the works of the law written in one's heart (Rom. 2:14-15). True Christianity is the death of the old man, who was born in sin, and receives the birth of a new life according to Romans 6:3-6. 2 Cor. 5:17 states, **"Therefore if any man be in Christ, he is a new creature: old things are passed away; behold, all things are become new."**

By saying what is known as the sinner's prayer, which is not actually even taught in scripture, does not necessarily mean that one receives salvation. There are many things that need to be considered. First, a confession with the mouth without a true belief in the heart will not bring salvation. One can think (head knowledge) that the gospel message is true without having a true belief in his/her heart. The Greek word (pisteuo) translated for 'believe' has a much stronger meaning than our English word. It is not just to believe that something exists, but to completely entrust and commit oneself to what is believed in. Many professing Christians believe (in the English since) that Jesus exists, and that He is the Son of God, but are not committed to living an obedient Christian lifestyle. Many who confess that they are saved continue to walk in the lusts and sinful nature of the flesh, according to the course of this world (Eph. 2:2-3). These individuals need to question their salvation.

Salvation as Taught in the Parable of the Sower

The parable of the sower can give us some valuable insight (Mk. 4:3-20). We learn from this parable that the seed, which is sown, is the Word of God. The ground is the heart of those that hear the Word. We also learn that there are four types of ground upon which the seed is sown. There is ground that is by the wayside, stony ground, thorny ground, and good ground. The seed, or Word, which falls by the way side shows those who have no interest in the gospel and Satan immediately comes and takes away the Word that was sown in their hearts. The Word sown on stony ground shows those who RECEIVE THE WORD WITH GLADNESS, but as it cannot actually take root in a stony heart, it does not bring true salvation. These can be professing Christians who seem to endure when all is going well, but are offended and fall away during times of affliction or persecution. The seed, which is sown among the thorns, show those who hear the Word, but the Word is choked out by the cares of this world, the deceitfulness of riches, and the lusts of other things. Many of these also profess to be Christians, but live worldly lives, caring far more for the things of this world than that which is to come. They just continue to live life for themselves much as they did before.

It is only the seed which is sown on the good ground that brings salvation. This shows the Word that falls upon a heart that has been prepared, ready, and willing to receive it. A heart that has been prepared will be softened through the working of the Holy Spirit; possibly through afflictions and trials or other circumstances in one's life. A person's heart that truly desires God is ready and willing to forsake this world. The Word must be planted and take root in the heart to bring forth a true belief in the gospel. When one truly believes in his heart, it will change the way he lives his life. A person WILL live his life according to what he truly believes in his heart. Therefore, the confession with the mouth of the Lord Jesus must come from the Word planted in the heart, and be spoken under the influence of the Holy Spirit. 1 Cor. 12:3 states that NO MAN CAN SAY THAT JESUS IS LORD, BUT BY THE HOLY GHOST. It is only by the Holy Spirit that one can truly confess Jesus Christ as Lord.

The Natural Birth can teach us about the Spiritual Birth

Jesus spoke of salvation as the act of being born again. Jn. 3:3 states, **"Jesus answered and said unto him, Verily, verily, I say unto thee, Except a man be born again, he cannot see the kingdom of God."** This second birth is a work of God's Spirit. Jn. 3:5 states, **"Jesus answered, Verily, verily, I say unto thee, Except a man be born of water and of the Spirit, he cannot enter into the kingdom of God."** Being born of God's Spirit is the only way of entering into God's Kingdom. This takes place simultaneously. A person enters into God's kingdom when they are born of God's Spirit. It is interesting to note that the first words, recorded in scripture, spoken by both John the Baptist and our Lord Jesus Christ are **"repent: for the kingdom of heaven (God) is at hand"** (Matt. 3:1, 4:17). The apostle Paul also referred to the kingdom of God as righteousness, and peace, and joy IN the Holy Ghost (Rom. 14:17).

Jesus often used natural examples to teach about spiritual things. In John chapter three He used the natural example of birth to teach about salvation, which is in reality a second birth. Much of this chapter is a conversation that Jesus had with a Pharisee named Nicodemus. When Jesus informed Nicodemus that he needed to be born again, he immediately thought of his natural birth. This is what Jesus needed him to do to get his message across. The phrase born again has become so common in the church that many of us miss the true meaning. Our natural birth can teach us much about what it is to be born again of God's Spirit. Our natural birth is how we entered into this world. Once born into this world we immediately began to live the life we were born into. There was no going back to the life of darkness we previously lived in our mother's bellies. Everything changed. We were now able to see the world we were born into. We began to drink milk as our source of food. We began to learn and live our lives according to all that agreed with our nature.

Salvation is to be born (again) of God's Spirit. Just as our natural birth was a life changing experience, so also is our spiritual birth. Our spiritual birth is how we enter into God's kingdom. This is not the physical kingdom that will be manifested at Jesus' second coming. When demanded of the Pharisees when the kingdom of God should come, Jesus stated, **"The kingdom of God cometh not with observation: Neither shall they say, Lo here! Or, lo there! for, behold, the kingdom of God is within you"** (Lk. 20-21). This must be in reference to the indwelling of the Holy Spirit.

We will find that God's Word often refers to the Holy Spirit when speaking of God's kingdom. Scripture introduces us to John the Baptist, preaching, **"Repent ye: for the kingdom of heaven** (or God) **is at hand"** (Matt. 3:1-2). Then speaking of the One (Jesus) who was to establish the kingdom, he stated:

> **I indeed baptize you with water unto repentance: but he that cometh after me is mightier than I, whose shoes I am not worthy to bear: he shall baptize you with the Holy Ghost, and with fire** (Matt. 3:11).

John's water baptism was therefore to prepare the people to receive the baptism with the Holy Ghost. Just as John came to baptize with water, Jesus Christ came to baptize with the Holy Ghost. This is essential as scripture states that we are ALL BAPTIZED into the body of Christ BY GOD'S SPIRIT (1 Cor. 12:13).

One cannot be born of God's Spirit and continue to just live life as before. Those born of God's Spirit are chosen (called) out of this present evil world, delivered from the power of darkness, and translated into the kingdom of Jesus Christ (Jn. 15:19, Gal. 1:4, Col. 1:13). Upon being born again, one immediately begins to live life in God's kingdom. Salvation is accompanied with a love for God and His children, a hunger for His Word, and a desire to live holy. These things are brought forth from God's Spirit which imparts to us the divine nature of God (2 Pet. 1:4). Sin disagrees with the divine nature and grieves the Holy Spirit. Sin brings conviction to one who is truly saved prompting them to turn from it. 1 Jn. 3:8-9 states:

> **He that committeth sin is of the devil; for the devil sinneth from the beginning. For this purpose the Son of God was manifested, that he might destroy the works of the devil. Whosoever is born of God doth not commit sin; for his seed remaineth in him: and he cannot sin, because he is born of God.**

The KJV of the bible puts an 'eth' on the end of the word commit because it is an ongoing verb (in the Greek). It speaks of having a commitment to sin. Those who have a commitment to sin are of the devil, but those born of God cannot have a commitment to sin. They can never sin as they did before salvation. Those who can continue to speak corruptly, commit sexual sins, steal, or any other thing that God's Word declares to be sin are most likely not saved. Especially, those who have little or no conviction, and those who do not strive to get the sin out of their lives.

People who have a commitment to sin have never come to true repentance. Without repentance there is no possibility of salvation. The word repent is translated from the Greek word 'metanoia'. It means to have a change of mind, a reversal. The Hebrew verb 'shub' expresses the Hebrew concept of NT repentance. It means to turn or return, which speaks of a change of direction. True repentance is a change of mind that changes one's direction. God does not save anyone to continue to live a sinful lifestyle. That is not what salvation is about. Jesus Christ came to save His people from their sins (Matt. 1:21). The word 'save' means to deliver, rescue, heal, etc. Sin does not have dominion over God's people that they should continue therein (Rom.6:1-14). According to God's Word, those who continue a sinful lifestyle are not saved.

Scriptural Examples of Salvation

So what is it to be born of God's Spirit? God's Word gives us examples throughout the book of Acts. The book of Acts begins approximately forty days after Jesus was resurrected from the dead. During these forty days He showed Himself to be alive to His disciples by many infallible proofs, and spoke to them of the things pertaining to God's kingdom. He instructed them to go to Jerusalem and wait for THE PROMISE of the Father, which was to be baptized with the Holy Spirit. He then ascended in a cloud into heaven (Acts 1:2-11).

The First Jewish Converts

The events of Acts chapter two took place ten days later on the day of Pentecost. Acts 2:1-4 states:

> **And when the day of Pentecost was fully come, they were all with one accord in one place. And suddenly there came a sound from heaven as of a rushing mighty wind, and it filled all the house where they were sitting. And there appeared unto them cloven tongues like as of fire, and it sat upon each of them. And they were all filled with the Holy Ghost, and began to speak with other tongues, as the Spirit gave them utterance.**

There are some important things we need to see here. God is not the author of confusion, but does all things decently and in order (1 Cor. 14:33, 40). The day of Pentecost has great significance. We can trace it all the way back to when Israel arrived at Mount Sinai after being delivered from Egypt. Scripture records that they arrived at Mount Sinai in the same time period that they were later instructed to celebrate the feast of Pentecost (Ex. 19:1). This is where they received the covenant of the law, also known as the Torah. (Torah means the teaching of God's instructions.) The timing of this feast was very important. They were to kill the Passover lamb on the fourteenth day of the first month of Abib, also known as the month of Nisan. The day following the next Sabbath, after the Passover, they were instructed to offer a wave sheaf of the barley harvest unto the Lord as the first fruits of the harvest. They were then to count fifty days, which began the feast of Pentecost. This feast was a celebration of the bringing in of the wheat harvest, and also commemorated the giving of the covenant of the law (Torah) at Mount Sinai.

All of this pointed to Jesus Christ and the church. Jesus was the Lamb of God who was killed at Passover to take away the sins of the world (Jn. 1:29). Three days later, on the day following the next Sabbath (the first day of the week), He rose from the dead as the first fruits of God's harvest. Then fifty days later, on the day of Pentecost, He sent the promise of the Holy Spirit. This is why the church is often spoken of as God's wheat harvest (Matt. 3:12, 13:24-30, 36-43). This was the birth of the NT church. This was the establishment of the New Covenant where God put His Spirit within His people, and His law was written in their hearts rather than on tables of stone (Jer. 31:31-34, Heb. 8:8-12, Ezek. 11:19-20, 36:25-27). The first four verses of Acts chapter two records the account of the first people to be born of God's Spirit. This was their salvation experience.

We also see from this passage of scripture (Acts 2:1-4) that the Holy Spirit came from heaven as a rushing mighty wind. There is also great significance in this. It goes all the way back to the creation of man when God breathed into Adam the breath of life (Gen. 2:7).

Many believe that the baptism with the Holy Spirit is a separate experienced from salvation, a second work of grace, and (or) is not given to everyone. None of which line up with God's Word or are even mentioned in scripture. Many teach these things because they believe that the disciples received the Holy Spirit when Jesus breathed on them, and said, **"Receive ye the Holy Ghost"** (Jn. 20:22). If this were true there would have been no need for them to go to Jerusalem and wait for the Holy Spirit, nor would there have been any need for the Holy Spirit to be sent down from heaven at a later time, nor would the day of Pentecost have any real significance. Jesus was just revealing to His disciples how the Holy Spirit was going to come. The rushing mighty wind was the breath of God breathing out His Spirit upon those in the upper room.

The cloven tongues of fire that sat upon each of them are also very significant. According to the Torah, an animal with a cloven hoof and chewed the cud was clean and could be eaten. The cloven tongues revealed to these Jewish disciples that this was clean and they were to receive it. As these cloven tongues of fire sat upon each of them they all spoke in other tongues (languages) as the Spirit gave them utterance. This reveals what we should expect to take place when we receive the Holy Spirit. This event has brought much confusion to many since the day it first took place. Peter explained it to the multitude that gathered together, by saying:

> **But this is that which was spoken by the prophet Joel; And it shall come to pass in the last days, saith God, I will pour out of my Spirit upon all flesh: and your sons and your daughters shall prophesy, and your young men shall see visions, and your old men shall dream dreams: and on my servant and on my handmaidens I**

will pour out in those days (not day) of my Spirit; and they shall prophesy** (Joel 2:28-29, Acts 2:16-18).

Peter referred to them speaking in tongues as the prophesying that those would do when God's Spirit was poured out upon them. The word 'prophesy' is translated from the Greek word 'propheteou'. It means to foretell events, divine, exercise the prophetic office, (or as in this case) to speak under inspiration. To speak in other tongues as the Spirit gives the utterance is to prophesy. This should not be confused with the gift of tongues spoken of in 1 Corinthians chapters twelve through fourteen. This is not the GIFT of DIVERS KINDS of tongues, but the SIGN of NEW tongues that are to follow every believer (Mk. 16:17-18). Few, if any, has every gift spoken of in 1 Corinthians 12:4-11, but all the signs spoken of in Mark 16:17-18 should follow every believer.

The fire spoken of in Acts 2:3 revealed that this was the Holy Spirit, as John spoke of them being baptized with the Holy Ghost, and with fire (Matt. 3:11). Scripture also refers to God as a consuming fire and would dwell in His people (Heb. 12:29, 2 Cor. 6:16).

The book of Acts is the only book in the NT that gives us actual accounts of people receiving the Holy Spirit. In all four accounts God's Word refers to an outward manifestation as a sign or indication of their having received salvation by being born of God's Spirit. Although Acts chapter two is the only place where these physical signs of the rushing mighty wind and tongues of fire appeared, the outward manifestation seen in those who received the Spirit remain the same.

The First Samaritan Converts

Acts chapter 8 records the account of the Samaritans receiving the Holy Spirit. This is the only account where scripture does not specify what the outward manifestation was, but definitely refers to something that could be seen. Acts 8:18 states, **"And when Simon SAW that through laying on of the apostles' hands the Holy Ghost was given."** (Capitals added for emphasis.) As the other three accounts all refer to speaking in tongues as the outward sign, there is no reason to think that the Samaritans experienced anything different.

The First Gentile Converts

Acts chapter 10-11 gives us the account of the first Gentiles to receive salvation. Acts chapter 10 introduces us to a Gentile man by the name of Cornelius. Each one of us should study this very carefully. God's Word refers to this man as a devout man, a man that feared God, gave alms, and prayed to God always (Acts 10:1-2). If this were all that was written about him we could easily come to the conclusion that he was already saved. However, as we read further we find that this was not the case. God sent an angel to Cornelius instructing him to send for Simon Peter (the lead apostle). As the messengers from Cornelius were on the way to find Peter, God gave Peter a vision to prepare him to preach the gospel to the Gentiles. Peter was then instructed by God's Spirit to go with the messengers who escorted him to Cornelius' house. After having come to the understanding of the vision, Peter proceeded to preach the gospel unto them. Acts 10:44-46 then states:

> **While Peter yet spake these words, the Holy Ghost fell on all them which heard the word. And they of the circumcision which believed were astonished, as many as came with Peter, because that on the Gentiles also was poured out the gift of the Holy Ghost. For they heard them speak with tongues and magnify God.**

Listen to what God's Word says. The Jews knew that the Holy Ghost was poured out upon the Gentiles FOR (or because) they heard them speak with tongues, and magnify God. Would not the same thing hold true today? Contrary to what many teach, there is nothing in God's Word that states anything different.

Many take 1 Corinthians 13:8-10 completely out of context in an attempt to teach that tongues have ceased. This passage of scripture states that prophecies shall fail, tongues shall cease, and knowledge shall pass away. We also learn from this passage of scripture that these things now exist because we know in part, and prophesy in part. These things are to fail, cease, and pass away when that which 'is perfect' is come. Many falsely believe that what Paul was referring to 'as perfect' was the New Testament. That cannot be possible. 1 Cor. 13:12 states, **"For now we see through a glass darkly; but then** (in reference to the time when that which is perfect has come) **face to face: now I know in part; but then shall I know even as also I am known."** Although the New Testament gives further insight, it does not change the fact that we NOW only know in part, or cause us to know even as we are known. It also does not cause prophecies to fail or knowledge to pass away. These things will not take place until the coming of Christ (see 1 Jn. 3:2). That which is perfect must be in reference to Jesus Christ.

Acts chapter 11 then records Peter's explanation of this to the apostles and brethren that were in Judea. Up to this time, the Jews were still under the impression that God's salvation would pertain only to Israel. Peter rehearsed everything that had taken place. He explained how God had instructed Cornelius to send for him, and that God's Spirit had instructed him to go to Cornelius, doubting nothing. Cornelius had then explained to Peter God's purpose for sending for him. Acts 11:14 states, **"Who (Peter) shall tell thee words, whereby thou and all thy house shall be saved."** So the man we are introduced to in chapter ten as a devout man, a man that feared God, gave alms, and prayed was as of yet unsaved. This is the same condition as thousands that fill churches all around the world. There are many devout God fearing people that have been taught all their lives that they do not need to be baptized with the Holy Spirit to be saved. Many churches even teach against it. Many are in the same spiritual state as Cornelius when we are first introduced to him in Acts chapter ten. Cornelius was not saved until he received the gift (baptism) of the Holy Spirit. As Cornelius, many just need to hear this message and cry out for God to save them according to the examples (or pattern) found in His Word.

Peter then went on to say,

> **And as I began to speak, the Holy Ghost fell on them, as on us at the beginning. Then remembered I the word of the Lord, how that he said, John indeed baptized with water; but ye SHALL be baptized with the Holy Ghost. Forasmuch then as God gave them the LIKE GIFT as he did unto us, who believed on the Lord Jesus Christ; what was I, that I could withstand God? When they heard these things, they held their peace, and glorified God, saying, Then hath God also to the Gentiles granted repentance unto life** (Acts 11:15-18). Capitals added for emphasis.

Each of us should carefully consider what God's Word says here. It states that the Holy Ghost fell on the Gentiles as it did on the Jews at the beginning. Nothing had changed. This was the baptism with the Holy Spirit that was promised to them. He goes on to say that God gave the Gentiles the LIKE GIFT as He did unto the Jews. Peter had previously informed Cornelius that God is no respecter of persons (Acts 10:34). They all received the like gift of salvation.

Uninformed Disciples of John the Baptist Converted

The other example is found in Acts 19:1-7. The apostle Paul had met about twelve of John the Baptist disciples who had not yet heard that the Holy Spirit was given. Paul expounded to them the fullness of the gospel. Laid his hand upon them, and they received the Holy Ghost. Once again, scripture records that they spoke with tongues, and prophesied. We should never deviate from God's Word. There are many who claim that this passed away with the first century church. That cannot be proven from scripture, and is shown to be false by the millions of believers who have had this same experience throughout the centuries. The Pentecostal churches are established upon this experience. There are also many who teach that this is not for everyone. Once again, that does not line up with the accounts recorded for us in God's Word. All that received the Holy Spirit received Him in like manner. How can any of us be absolutely sure of our salvation if the Holy Spirit does not fall upon us as it did on those at the beginning? This is God's method of salvation verified by three witnesses recorded in the book of Acts; the mouth of two or three witnesses establishes every word. (Deut. 19:15, Matt. 18:16).

This does not mean that everyone who does not speak in tongues is not saved. There are surely many who have truly repented and cried out to God for salvation that received the Holy Spirit without speaking in tongues. This is very possible due to all the different teachings that have infiltrated the church. God's Word does not say that we know them because they speak in tongues, but we know them by their fruits (Matt. 7:16, 20). However, this is an experience that each and every born again believer can and probable should have. According to your faith be it unto you (Matt. 9:29). Scripture does instruct each of us to build up ourselves on our most holy faith praying in the Holy Ghost (tongues, Jude 20).

This is something that is between each believer and God. Each of us needs to be sure we will not be among the many who think they are saved, but are not. What better way than to have the same experience and follow the same pattern recorded for us in God's Word; and join the countless others who have had this same experience throughout the centuries. We each need to work out our OWN salvation with fear and trembling, and give diligence to make our calling and election sure (Phil. 2:12, 2 Pet. 1:10).

Chapter 2

LIKE FATHER LIKE SON (OR DAUGHTER)

Most all of us have heard the old sayings: like father like son, or like mother like daughter. This is because a child will almost always resemble their parents, and will act much like them. This is a very natural occurrence because children come forth from the bodies of their parents, and are therefore in their image and likeness (Gen. 5:3).

Most born again believers do not fully realize what God did in their lives upon salvation. God's Word tells us that we were predestinated unto the adoption of children by Jesus Christ unto God the Father (Eph. 1:5). Romans 8:15 also tells us that we have received the Spirit of adoption, whereby we cry, Abba, Father.

The problem is that many believers look at their relationship with God as that of an adopted child as it would be according to the flesh. An adopted child, according to the flesh, does not come out of the loins of the one he or she knows as their father. What makes someone a legitimate child of their father is that they came out of his loins, by being born of his seed. A child is a part of their father. They are what he is.

Every Seed Brings Forth After His Own Kind

That is what God was after all along. If God was ever to have true sons and daughters, it would be necessary for them to come out of God Himself, and be born from His seed. God begins to teach us this right from Genesis chapter one. It is here that the Word first teaches us about SEED, one of the most important topics (if not the most important) taught in scripture. Gen. 1:11-12 states:

> **And God said, Let the earth bring forth grass, the herb yielding seed, and the fruit tree yielding fruit after his kind, whose seed is in itself, upon the earth: and it was so. And the earth brought forth grass, and herb yielding seed after his kind, and tree yielding fruit, whose seed was in itself, after his kind: and God saw that it was good.**

We learn from these scriptures that every plant God created has his seed in itself, and brings forth after his own kind. To put it simply, it produces what it is. An apple seed brings forth an apple tree, a grass seed brings forth a blade of grass, etc. Genesis 1:21, 24-25 then states:

> **And God created great whales, and every living creature that moveth, which the waters brought forth abundantly, after their kind, and every winged foul after his kind: and God saw that it was good. And God said, Let the earth bring forth the living creature after his kind, cattle, and creeping thing, and beast of the earth after his kind: and it was so. And God made the beast of the earth after his kind, and cattle after their kind, and everything that creepeth upon the earth after his kind, and God saw that it was good.**

So what is true with all plant life is also true of all animal life. God created everything with his seed in itself, with everything bringing forth after their own kind. Cattle bring forth cattle, ducks bring forth ducks, fish bring forth fish, etc.

Now look at what the very next verse says, **"And God said, Let us make man in our image, after our likeness"** (Gen. 1:26a). For God to truly make man in His image and after His likeness, man would have to come out of God and be born of His seed. This was not true with the first man, Adam. He was not born of God's seed, but was formed from the dust of the earth (Gen. 2:7).

The question that should now come into our minds is, "How is a man born of God's seed?" In order to understand this one must understand the parable of the sower. This was the first parable that Jesus taught because it holds the key to understand all the other parables, and to know the mystery of the kingdom of God (Mk. 4:11-13). This concept of what the Word teaches on SEED is vitally important. God even set up Israel as an agricultural community so they might understand the importance of this subject matter. The parable of the sower is found in three of the 4 gospels. (Matt. 13:3-23, Mk. 4:3-20, Lk. 8:5-18). Each account begins with a sower going out to sow seed. The gospel of Matthew speaks of the seed as the Word of the kingdom (Matt. 13:19). Mark speaks of the sower sowing the Word (Mk 4:14). The gospel of Luke says, **"The seed is the word of God"** (Lk. 8:11). God's Word is His seed. It is what came forth from His essence and births His children into His kingdom. God's seed is sown into the hearts of men as His Word is taught and preached. 1 Peter 1:23 states, **"Being born again, not of corruptible seed, but of incorruptible, by the word of God, which liveth and abideth forever."** (Underlining of some words have been added for emphasis.)

Concerning salvation, it is very common to hear Romans 10:9-10 quoted. However, little to no attention is usually given to verse eight, which must come prior to the events spoken of in the following verses:

> **But what saith it? The word is nigh thee, even in thy mouth, and in thy heart: that is, the word of faith, which we preach;** (Rom. 10:8) **That if thou shalt confess with thy mouth the Lord Jesus, and shalt believe in thy heart that God hath raised him from the dead, thou shalt be saved. For with the heart man believeth unto righteousness; and with the mouth confession is made unto salvation** (Rom. 10:9-10).

The Word must enter into a heart prepared as good soil in the same way that a farmer prepares the ground to receive the seed he is planting. As Jesus taught in the parable of the sower, many people hear the Word without receiving salvation. It is because the Word falls on hearts that have not been prepared to receive it, preventing the Word from being planted in their hearts. Even though God holds the ultimate role in preparing our hearts, we are not left without any responsibility in this process. 1 Sam. 7:3 states:

> **And Samuel spake unto all the house of Israel, saying, If ye do return unto the LORD with all your hearts, then put away the strange gods and Ashtaroth from among you, and prepare your hearts unto the LORD, and serve him only: and he will deliver you out of the hand of the Philistines.**

We also learn that King Rehoboam did evil because he did not prepare his heart to seek the LORD (2 Chron. 12:14). 2 Chron. 20:33 also states, **"Howbeit the high places were not taken away: for as yet the people had not prepared their hearts unto the God of their fathers."** We are instructed to sow in righteousness, and break up our fallow ground (Hosea 10:12).

Many want salvation on their own terms. They desire to keep their belief silent so as not to suffer persecution, and are not willing to give up certain sins or things of this world; all of which show a hard, thorn filled heart. An unprepared heart will not endure persecution or tribulation for the Word's sake, nor is it willing to forsake the cares and riches of this world (see Mk. 4:14-20). When the Word is not sown in the good soil of the heart, no confession with the mouth will bring salvation. The confession from the mouth of the Lord Jesus must come from the Word that has entered into the heart.

Jesus Christ is God's Word, God's Seed

The Word sown in the heart produces the confession of the Lord Jesus Christ because they are one and the same. We can never separate God's Word from Jesus Christ. When speaking in reference to Jesus, John 1:1 & 1:14 states:

> **In the beginning was the Word, and the Word was with God, and the Word was God (vs. 1). And the Word was made flesh, and dwelt among us, (and we beheld his glory, the glory as of the only begotten of the Father,) full of grace and truth.**

Scriptures also speaks of the resurrected Christ as the Word of life, and His name is called the Word of God (1 Jn. 1:1, Rev. 19:13). When we receive the Word, we are receiving Jesus Christ Himself. This is what the apostle Paul called the mystery that was hid from ages and generations; which is Christ in you, the hope of glory (Col. 1:26-27).

It is the Word that forms Christ in us (Gal. 4:19), that grows us up into Him (Eph. 4:15), and conforms us into His image (Rom. 8:29). As newborn babes we are to desire the sincere milk of the Word, that we may grow thereby (1 Peter 2:2). We are then able to receive the meat of the Word, and grow to maturity. We are what we eat. It is no wonder that God puts so much importance on His Word. His Words are spirit and life (Jn. 6:63). His word is life unto those that find them, and health to all their flesh (Pro. 4:22). He told Israel:

Set your hearts unto all the words which I testify among you this day, which ye shall command your children to observe and do, all the words of this law. For it is not a vain thing for you; because it is your life (Deut. 32: 46-47a).

Jesus Christ was that very law (Torah) made flesh. Being born of God's Word, which is His seed, makes one just as much a son/daughter of God as they are a child of their natural father.

Chapter 3

A NEW BEGINNING

Jesus spoke of salvation as being born again (Jn. 3:1-6). A birth always speaks of a new life. The book of Titus calls it the washing of regeneration, and renewing of the Holy Ghost (Titus 3:5). Regeneration is to generate again. To generate is to bring into being or to begin. To renew is to make new. Salvation is the regeneration of those who were born dead in trespasses and sins, so that they are quickened and given spiritual life (Eph. 2:1). It is to be delivered from this world, and translated (placed) into the kingdom of Jesus Christ (Gal. 1:4, Col. 1:13). It is to be changed from a child of the devil into a child of God (Jn. 8:44, Eph. 2:2-3, 1 Jn. 3:8-10, Jn. 1:12).

Salvation is a new beginning. It is the start of a new and unending life. This is seen throughout scripture. For instance, when God delivered the nation of Israel out of Egypt, which is a type of salvation, He told them, **"This month shall be unto you the beginning of months: it shall be the first month of the year to you"** (Ex. 12:2). This was the month of Abib, which means 'green ears' and speaks of new life. The term Abib is from an unused root meaning: to be tender, green, i.e. a young ear of grain, or newly developed grain. It later also became known as the month of Nisan which means beginning, or opening.

A Covenant Relationship

Upon salvation we enter into a covenant relationship with God. As usual, the Old Covenant gives us a wonderful example of this. During the time of the Old Testament, a man entered into covenant with God when he was circumcised on the eighth day of his life. The circumcision was the sign of the covenant (Gen. 17:9-13). The number 8 represents a new beginning. It is two connected unending circles, which also speak of everlasting life.

Speaking in reference to the second coming of our Lord, 2 Pet. 2:8 states, **"But, beloved, be not ignorant of this one thing, that one day is with the Lord as a thousand years, and a thousand years as one day."** Many biblical scholars believe that the bible covers a time period of around seven thousand years. The circumcision on the eighth day of a man's life points to the eight thousandth year, which only those in covenant with God will enter into. This is when death, the last enemy, will be destroyed (see 1 Cor. 15:23-28).

A New Creation

Our new birth is a creative life giving work of God's Spirit. Each born again believer enters into, and becomes a member of the body of Christ (1 Cor. 12: 12-27). 2 Cor. 5:17 states, **"Therefore if any man be in Christ, he is a new creature: old things have passed away; behold, all things are become new."** Consider this, when we speak of something or someone passing away we are speaking of his or her death. Salvation is the death of the old man, who was born dead in trespasses and sins (Eph. 2:1), and the birth of a new creature in Christ Jesus.

God's Word gives more clarity to this in the book of Romans.

> **Know ye not, that so many of us as were baptized into Jesus Christ were baptized into his death? Therefore we are buried with him by baptism into death: that**

> **like as Christ was raised up from the dead by the glory of the Father, even so we also should walk in newness of life. For if we have been planted together in the likeness of his death, we shall be also in the likeness of his resurrection: Knowing this, that our old man is crucified with him, that the body of sin might be destroyed, that henceforth we should not serve sin. For he that is dead is freed from sin** (Rom. 6:3-7).

The whole purpose of crucifixion was to put someone to death. There was absolutely nothing symbolic about the death of Jesus Christ. He suffered a literal, physical death on the cross. He was buried, and then resurrected from the dead. This is exactly what takes place in our lives when we come unto salvation. Our old man is crucified with Jesus and put to death. We are then buried with Him by baptism into death. This means the old man really died, as one only buries that which is dead. As we have been planted together in the likeness of His death, the same holds true with His resurrection. Just as Christ was raised up from the dead, we are also raised up into newness of life in Him.

Nothing we have ever done in the past can or will be held against us by God. That man, our old nature, has died and we are now justified in Christ. Few of us actually realize the fullness of what it really means to be justified. Justification is a term in reference to a judicial judgment. Many seem to understand it to be like a pardon, but it is not. A pardon is the exemption of a convicted person from the penalties of his crime by a high-ranking official. It allows forgiveness for an offense that he or she has committed. Someone pardoned for murder is a pardoned murderer. To justify is not to pardon one from his sins, nor is it to make one righteous. It is to acquit and declare righteous. It is to prove that one is just, right, and free of blame. This is because the old man died, and the new creature in Christ is acquitted and declared righteous from anything the old man committed. Salvation gives us a second chance and a new beginning.

Chapter 4

WHAT'S IN YOUR HOUSE

Now there cried a certain woman of the wives of the sons of the prophets unto Elisha, saying, Thy servant my husband is dead; and thou knowest that thy servant did fear the LORD: and the creditor is come to take unto him my two sons to be bondmen. And Elisha said unto her, What shall I do for thee? tell me, what hast thou in the house? And she said, Thine handmaid hath not anything in the house, save a pot of oil. Then he said, Go, borrow thee vessels abroad of all thy neighbours, even empty vessels; borrow not a few. And when thou art come in, thou shalt shut the door upon thee and upon thy sons, and shalt pour out into all those vessels, and thou shalt set aside that which is full. So she went from him, and shut the door upon her and upon her sons, who brought the vessels to her; and she poured out. And it came to pass, when the vessels were full, that she said unto her son, Bring me yet a vessel. And he said unto her, There is not a vessel more. And the oil stayed. Then she came and told the man of God. And he said, Go, sell the oil, and pay thy debt, and live thou and thy children of the rest (2 Ki. 4:1-7).

There is a very powerful message behind these verses of scripture. This widow woman came to Elisha the prophet in great need. He then asked her the question, "WHAT HAST THOU IN THE HOUSE?" She had nothing but one pot of oil that she apparently seen as having little value. Elisha then told her to go and borrow an abundance of empty vessels, shut the door upon her and her sons, and fill the vessels from the pot of oil. The pot of oil filled every vessel she borrowed without running dry, and gave her enough not only to pay her debt, but also to live on. This woman unknowingly possessed something that would abundantly supply all her needs, and much more.

The Overflowing Power of God's Spirit

Throughout scripture, oil is always symbolic of the Holy Spirit. A believer's body is spoken of as a house (2 Cor. 5:1-4) or temple where the Holy Spirit abides (1 Cor. 3:16-17, 6:19-20). There are many believers who do not realize what they have, or the value and power of the Holy Spirit. They see the Holy Spirit as having little value when it comes to their physical needs to live this life. The real truth is that those who have God's Spirit possess that which is able to abundantly supply all their needs, and much more.

So, how does one experience the overflowing abundance of God's Spirit, and what He has to offer? Let's look closer at this passage of scripture. This widow woman received this blessing as a result of her late husbands 'fear' of the Lord, which she must have also shared. When the Old Testament speaks of the fear of the Lord, it is in reference to a reverential trust in God, and a hatred and departure from evil (Pro. 3:7, 8:13, 16:6). First and foremost, a person must live a holy life for the power of the Holy Ghost to flow in and through their life.

A person must also have a strong prayer life. This woman going into her house, and shutting the door upon her and her sons, is a type of entering into her prayer closet (Matt. 6:6). Whatever we receive from God we receive through a prayer of faith. Even though God knows what we need even before we ask Him, we are still to ask (Matt. 6:8). A person must also believe God's Word, put it into practice, and not limit the power of God. This woman received God's Word, (spoken by His prophet,) and acted upon it. When you receive the prophet's word, you also receive a prophet's reward. In the natural it would seem ridiculous to go and borrow far more vessels than the pot of oil could possibly fill. Many believers never experience the supernatural power of God because they only consider the natural circumstance, which is often contrary to God's Word. Most do not really believe that God can or will make the impossible possible. Just because it is impossible for man does not mean that it is impossible for God (Mk. 10:27). There is no limit to the overflowing power of the Holy Spirit, but God will not go beyond what we have the faith to believe Him for. The pot of oil filled as many vessels as the woman borrowed, but could have continued indefinitely.

This is also a type of God's Spirit, in all His power, filling every born again believer whose bodies are spoken of as earthen vessels (2 Cor. 4:7). There is a prayer in the book of Ephesians that we should all include in our own prayers:

> **For this cause I bow my knees unto the Father of our Lord Jesus Christ. Of whom the whole family in heaven and earth is named, That he would grant you, according to the riches of his glory, to be strengthened with might by his Spirit in the inner man; That Christ may dwell in your hearts by faith; that ye, being rooted and grounded in love, May be able to comprehend with all saints what is the breadth, and length, and depth, and height; and to know the love of Christ, which passeth knowledge, that ye might be filled with all the fullness of God** (Eph. 3:14-19).

Just to focus in on a portion of this important prayer, we are to pray for God to strengthen us with might by His Spirit in our inner man. So, just because someone has God's Spirit does not necessarily mean that he is being strengthened by Him. Those who are strengthened 'with might' by God's Spirit will experience the power of God in their lives.

The verse that immediately follows this prayer, says, "**Now unto him that is able to do exceeding abundantly above all that we ask or think, according to the power that worketh in us**" (Eph. 3:20). The power that works in us is the power of the Holy Spirit. This means that there is absolutely nothing that we even have the ability to ask or think that God cannot perform through the power of His Spirit within us. The biggest and greatest thing that we can even possibly imagine to ask God to do, is but a small thing for Him to perform.

We should never put any limitations upon God or the working of the Holy Spirit in our lives. The Word states that those whom God delivered out of Egypt limited the Holy One of Israel (Ps. 78:41). Luke 1:37 tells us, "**For with God nothing shall be impossible**." Jesus also told us, "**If thou canst believe, all things are possible to him that believeth**" (Mark. 9:23). We can believe through the power of the Holy Spirit if He is in our house.

Chapter 5

PUTTING GOD FIRST

God should be the first and foremost important thing in a believer's life. We should love Him and value our relationship with Him above all else. When Jesus was asked which the greatest commandment was in the law or Torah, He replied, **"Thou shalt love the Lord thy God with all thy heart, and with all thy soul, and with all thy mind. This is the first and great commandment"** (Matt. 37-38).

Even though it should be our hearts desire to love God above all else, and put Him first in our lives, it is not without its rewards. Actually, most Christians live far below the benefits, privileges, and blessings that are available to them because they do not put God first in their lives. Too many of us get so caught up in living this life that God is not even close to being on top of our list of priorities. Most of us work harder to lay up for ourselves treasures upon the earth, rather than to lay up for ourselves treasures in heaven (Matt. 6:19-20). Many of us continually take thought and labor for food, clothes, cars, houses, and lands. We think and labor for these things more than for heavenly things because of a lack of faith for God to supply these needs, as well as an ungodly love for this world. Concerning all the things we need to live this life,

Matt. 6:33, which states, "**But seek ye first the kingdom of God, and his righteousness; and all these things shall be added unto you.**"

Examples of Putting God First

God is a supernatural wonder working God; especially for those who put Him first and trust Him regardless of any situation or circumstance. Let's look at some examples in God's Word beginning with King Solomon. The Word states that Solomon loved the Lord and walked in the statutes of David his father. Shortly after beginning his reign as king over Israel, he offered a thousand burnt offerings unto the Lord. The Lord then appeared unto him in a dream, and said, "**Ask what I shall give thee**" (1 Ki. 3:3-5). Take notice that God left it wide open. He put no limitations or restrictions on what Solomon could ask for. Why would God have such confidence in Solomon? For one thing, Solomon put God first by walking in obedience to His Word. Jn. 15:7 states, "**If ye abide in me, and my words abide in you, ye shall ask what ye will, and it shall be done unto you.**" If a person truly abides (lives) in Christ, and God's Word abides in them, whatever they ask is going to be according to the Word that dwells in them. They will desire to please God. He also dedicated and consecrated himself to God with a thousand burnt offerings, which is the number of the millennial reign of God's kingdom (Remember Matt. 6:33).

Solomon then asked God for an understanding heart (wisdom) to judge His people so that he would be able to discern between good and bad. God was very pleased in what Solomon ask for, and responded by saying:

> **Because thou hast asked this thing, and hast not asked for thyself long life; neither hast asked riches for thyself, nor hast asked the life of thine enemies; but hast asked for thyself understanding to discern judgment; Behold, I have done according to thy words: lo, I have given thee a wise and an understanding heart; so that there was none like thee before thee,**

> **neither after thee shall any arise like unto thee. And I have also given thee that which thou hast not asked, both riches, and honour: so that there shall not be any among the kings like unto thee all thy days. And if thou wilt walk in my ways, to keep my statutes and my commandments, as thy father David did walk, then I will lengthen thy days (1 Kings 3:11-14).**

Solomon sought first the things that pertained to the kingdom of Israel (God's kingdom), and all other things were added unto him. He reigned for forty years with all the surrounding nations subject to his kingdom. He also became the wealthiest king that ever reigned over Israel.

There are sacrifices we will need to make, and things we will need to give up in order to put God first in our lives. Many Christians are unwilling to do so. MANY seem to believe that God just asks too much of them, and are under the impression that God desires His people to be poor in this life. Nothing could be farther from the truth. God desires our priorities to be right so that we put nothing before Him. Once God takes first place in our lives, the blessings are far more than most of us even imagine. God will never ask us to give up anything that will not greatly benefit us, and He will always have something far better for us.

The Rich Young Ruler

For example, a rich young ruler came to Jesus and asked what he needed to do to inherit eternal life. Jesus told him to keep the commandments. The young man stated that he had done so from his youth. Jesus then told him that he yet lacked one thing. He instructed him to go and sell all that he had and give it to the poor, and he would have treasure in heaven. He was then to come, take up his cross, and follow him (Jesus). The man went away sad because he had great possessions. Jesus then stated that it was easier for a camel to go through the eye of a needle than for a rich man to enter into the kingdom of God (Mk. 10:17-25).

> **Upon seeing and hearing this, Peter said unto Jesus, Lo, we have left all, and have followed thee. Jesus responded by saying, Verily I say unto you, There is no man that hath left house, or brethren, or sisters, or father, or mother, or wife, or children, or lands, for my sake, and the gospel's, But he shall receive an hundredfold now in this time, houses, and brethren, and sisters, and mothers, and children, and lands, with persecutions; and in the world to come eternal life** (Mk. 10:28-30).

Being rich of itself keeps no one from entering God's kingdom. The bible speaks of many great men of God being very wealthy. Look at Abraham, David, Solomon, and Job just to name a few. God blessed all of these men with riches and wealth. They had their priorities in the right place with God. Being rich hinders most because they will usually trust in their riches, and put their riches before God. Concerning the rich, God's Word states:

> **Charge them that are rich in this world, that they be not high-minded, nor trust in uncertain riches, but in the living God, who giveth us richly all things to enjoy; That they do good, that they be rich in good works, ready to distribute, willing to communicate; Laying up in store for themselves a good foundation against the time to come, that they may lay hold on eternal life"** (1 Tim. 6:17-19).

Elijah and the Widow Woman

God's Word gives us another excellent example of the great benefits of putting God first as seen with the widow woman who received the prophet Elijah into her house during a time of severe famine in the land. When Elijah approached this woman he asked her for a morsel of bread. She responded by saying:

As the LORD thy God liveth, I have not a cake, but an handful of meal in a barrel, and a little oil in a cruse: and, behold, I am gathering two sticks, that I may go in and dress it for me and my son, that we may eat it and die." Elijah then said unto her, **"Fear not; go and do as thou hast said: but make me thereof a little cake first, and bring it unto me, and after make for thee and for thy son. For thus saith the LORD God of Israel, The barrel of meal shall not waste, neither shall the cruse of oil fail, until the day that the LORD sendeth rain upon the earth** (1 Ki. 17:12-14).

Elijah made it a point to say unto her that she was to make him a cake FIRST, and AFTER make for her and her son. Scripture clearly teaches that what we do for God's people we also do for God (Matt. 10:40-42, 25:34-40, Mk. 9:41, Heb. 6:10). She received Elijah as a prophet of God, and at God's Word put him first before her and her son. As a result they all ate of that same barrel of meal and cruse of oil until the famine was over.

Elisha and the Firstfruits

During the time that Elisha was a prophet in Israel, a man brought unto him twenty barley loaves and full ears of corn of the first fruits. The nation of Israel was always instructed to give God the first and the best of all their increase (Num. 18:12-13, 29). Elisha then instructed that the food be given to the people for them to eat. His servant informed him that it was not nearly enough to set before an hundred men. Elisha then said, **"Give the people, that they may eat: for thus saith the LORD, They shall eat and leave thereof"** (2 Ki. 42-44). This increase was according to the blessings that one receives when putting God first, and giving Him of the first fruits of all our substance. Proverbs 3:9-10 states, **"Honour the LORD with thy substance, and with the first fruits of all thine increase: So shall thy barns be filled with plenty, and thy presses shall burst out with new wine."**

We should also put God first by giving Him the first and best of each day. We should rise up early enough each morning to spend time with Him in prayer, and in the study of His Word. If we seek Him first at the start of each day, all things we need will be added to our lives.

Chapter 6

EXERCISE THYSELF UNTO GODLINESS

But refuse profane and old wives' fables, and EXERCISE THYSELF RATHER UNTO GODLINESS. For bodily exercise profiteth little: but godliness is profitable unto all things, having promise of the life that now is, and of that which is to come (1 Tim. 4:7-8). (Capital letters added for emphasis.)

God has set up many things in the natural to teach and instruct us about spiritual things. God's Word instructs us here to exercise ourselves unto godliness. This should let us know that to achieve godliness will require some work on our part. This should speak loudly to us today as there are so many who vigorously exercise to achieve and maintain good health, and to improve their physical appearance. Exercising our bodies makes them healthier, stronger, builds endurance, and makes them more fit and capable to perform physical activities. Those who achieve their goals must be serious, committed, faithful, and disciplined to their exercise routine. We will find that it works the same way spiritually.

It is surprising to find how many Christians are not committed to their spiritual life, or are more committed to their physical health than their spiritual. Don't get me wrong, our physical health is very important, and we should strive to do whatever is necessary to have and to keep it; but we should be even more committed to what we need to do spiritually. As God's Word uses bodily exercise as an example of exercising ourselves unto godliness, the one is to teach us about the other. The Word states that bodily exercise profits little: but godliness is profitable unto all things, having promise for this life, and the life to come. To put it more simply, bodily exercise profits us for a little time, in reference to our time on earth in this flesh; but godliness not only profits us now but also in the life to come.

A Healthy Diet of God's Word

Just as there are different types and ways to exercise our bodies, with each producing different results, there are also many things we need to do to exercise ourselves unto godliness. One of the most important things that a person must do to get desired results from any exercise program is to eat properly. Those who are serious about getting the most from their physical exercise eat the most nutritious foods. They also remove sugar and other junk food from their diet, for these types of food can actually work against what they are striving to achieve. God's Word is the spiritual man's proper and most healthy food. In order to attain godliness we must have a steady diet of God's Word. We must discipline ourselves to study God's Word daily, and at the same time remove the things from our diet (lives) that promote ungodliness. These can include (but are not limited to) worldly books, magazines, TV programs, and the worldly conversations that we far too often engage ourselves in. All of these things also feed us spiritually, but promote the things of the world and of the flesh, and therefore produce ungodliness.

Exercise Ourselves Through Prayer

Another way we exercise ourselves unto godliness is by prayer. Prayer is a labor that far too many of us neglect. Our flesh opposes God and does not have any desire to pray. It is so easy to give into that extra hour of sleep in the morning rather than getting up and spending that time in prayer, and then just as easy to neglect to pray throughout the day.

Jesus set a good example for us to follow. He would rise up early before daybreak to pray, and would often pray throughout the night (Mk. 1:35, Lk. 6:12). On the night before His crucifixion, He instructed His disciples to watch and pray that they would not enter into temptation. He informed them that the spirit was willing, but the flesh was weak. He prayed three separate times, each time returning to find His disciples asleep (Matt. 26:36-45). He received strength to help him endure the cross, but His disciples all forsook Him and fled (Lk. 22:43, Matt. 26:56). They all entered into temptation. Peter entered into the greatest temptation of all, resulting in him denying the Lord three times that same night.

Exercise Ourselves Through Fasting

We can also exercise ourselves unto godliness by fasting. Fasting is often necessary to receive deliverances from the strong holds in our lives (Mk. 9:29). Scripture records that God's people often fasted when they were in need of deliverance from sin or an attack of the enemy.

Unlike anything else fasting aids us to crucify the flesh, mortify the deeds of the body, and brings forth the strength and life of the Spirit at the same time. Each meal that is missed weakens the flesh. The flesh cannot walk by faith or please God in any way (Rom. 8:5-13). Many of the things that weaken or hinder our faith is suppressed or taken out of the way as we weaken the activity of the flesh through fasting. Fasting can increase our faith and add a turbocharge to our prayers. The study of God's Word and prayer should replace the natural meals and most other activities that we would usually participate in. This strengthens us to put off the corrupt lifestyle of the old man, be renewed in the spirit of our minds, and to put on the new man which after God is created in righteousness and true holiness (Eph. 4:22-24).

A Consistent Lifestyle

All of these things need to become a regular part of our spiritual lives. In the natural, those who remain in good condition do so because they continue to exercise. They make it a part of their lifestyle. If a weight lifter stops lifting he will slowly begin to lose the muscle mass and strength he obtained through his consistency. If a long distance runner stops training, he will also begin to lose the endurance and conditioning he obtained through his training. The bible teaches that it works the same way spiritually. The bible compares us to earthen vessels because the things we have received can and will leak out (2 Cor. 4:7, Heb. 2:1). If we go a long period of time without studying God's Word we will forget and lose much of what we had learned. Scriptures we memorized will become difficult or impossible to quote. We will forget where familiar passages of scripture are in the bible, and even much of what the bible teaches on certain subjects. The writer of the book of Hebrews warns us of this very thing:

> **Of whom we have many things to say, and hard to be uttered, seeing ye are dull of hearing. For when for the time ye ought to be teachers, ye have need that one teach you again which be the first principles of the oracles of God; and are become such as have need of milk, and not of strong meat. For every one that useth milk is unskillful in the word of righteousness: for he is a babe. But strong meat belongeth to them that are of full age, even those who by reason of use have their senses exercised to discern both good and evil** (Heb. 5:11).

The writer of the book of Hebrews desired to teach his readers about a hard subject matter (concerning Melchizedek), but was concerned about their ability to receive it as he seen they were dull of hearing. He informed them that they had been saved long enough that they should have been teachers of God's Word, but they had actually gone backwards. They were in need for someone to teach them AGAIN the first principles of God's Word. They had reverted back to being babes who were in need of the milk of God's Word rather than the strong meat, which is for those who have matured in Christ. The reason given is that they did not USE God's Word to have their senses EXERCISED to discern both good and evil. There is no such thing as standing still in Christ. We are either going forward or backward. We are either growing to maturity or reverting back to being a babe.

Natural Examples that Promote Spiritual Exercise

God's Word often compares our time on earth after salvation to that of a long distance runner. Heb. 12:1-2 states:

> **Wherefore seeing we also are compassed about with so great a cloud of witnesses, let us lay aside every weight, and the the sin which doth so easily beset us, and let us run with patience the race that is set before us, Looking unto Jesus the author and finisher of our faith; who for the joy that was set before him endured the cross, despising the shame, and is set down at the right hand of the throne of God.**

When running a long distance race it is important to be as light as possible. No runner is going to wear or carry anything that is going to slow him down or tire him out. He must also pace himself and patiently run the race.

What a perfect illustration of what we need to do spiritually. We need to condition ourselves by studying God's Word, praying, fasting, fellowship, etc. These things need to become a part of our lifestyles. We need to remove the things of the world that weigh us down and cause us to tire and grow weary as Christians. We need to understand that there are many things that we can involve ourselves in that are not sinful in themselves, but take up the time we need to spend with God. Those who spend little time with God are spiritually weak. This will make the Christian life seem hard and burdensome. We also need to obey God's Word and remove the sin that so easily steers us off course. Just as a runner looks to the finish line, we are to look unto Jesus by whom we began and will finish this race.

God's Word gives us another example in 1 Cor. 9:24-27:

> **Know ye not that they which run in a race run all, but one receiveth the prize? So run, that ye may obtain. And every man that striveth for the mastery is temperate in all things. Now they do it to obtain a corruptible crown; but we an incorruptible. I therefore so run, not as uncertainly; so fight I, not as one that beateth the air. But I keep under my body, and bring it into subjection: lest that by any means, when I have preached to others, I myself should be a castaway.**

Just as only one runner in a race receives the prize, we are to run with the attitude to be that one. We are to be temperate (or self-restrained) in all things. We are to be conditioned to endure to the end and obtain the prize of the incorruptible crown.

This passage of scripture also uses the illustration of a fighter. After all, we are called to spiritual warfare. The apostle Paul states here that he did not fight as one that beats the air (shadow boxing), so he is referring to a real opponent. Just as any natural fighter needs to be prepared and stay in condition for each fight, he also kept under his body and brought it into subjection. As the great men of God before us, we also need to exercise ourselves unto godliness, fight a good fight, finish our course, and keep the faith (2 Tim. 4:7).

Chapter 7

TRUE COMMITMENT

Commitment is a much stronger word than many of us realize. A true commitment is to be bound to an idea or course of action. An excellent illustration is that of an airplane on a runway. When an airplane is speeding down a runway for the purpose of taking flight, there is a period of time when the pilot has the option of aborting the flight. However, there does come a time and place on the runway when that option no longer exists and the plane must take off. The pilot then records the words, "I am committed." At that point he is committed to take off regardless of any unknown, unseen, or sudden circumstances that may surface. It does not matter if an engine fails or if the pilot realizes the wings are iced up. He is committed and must take off regardless of any circumstances. That's what it is to be truly committed.

A true commitment does not give the option of turning back, not following through, or taking another course of action. If one can even consider other options or another course of action, he has not made a true commitment. Although this type of commitment might be too rigid and inflexible in many circumstances, it is the type of commitment each one of us is called to concerning our walk with God.

Believers are to Follow the Committed Life of Jesus Christ

As always, Jesus Christ is our example to follow. 1 Pet. 2:21-24 states:

> **For even hereunto were ye called: because Christ also suffered for us, leaving us an example, that ye should follow his steps: Who did no sin, neither was guile found in his mouth: Who, when he was reviled, reviled not again; when he suffered, he threatened not; BUT COMMITTED HIMSELF to him that judgeth righteously: Who his own self bare our sins in his own body on the tree, that we, being dead to sins, should live unto righteousness: by whose stripes ye were healed.**

(Capitals added for emphasis.)

The Word states here that Jesus Christ committed Himself to God the Father. No amount of reviling or suffering could turn Him from His course of action as He was bound to it. He performed God's will even when it meant suffering severely and dying on the cross.

Far too many Christians are unwilling to suffer for their faith in Jesus Christ, which is a needed part of our salvation. A key theme in the book of 1 Peter is the suffering that Christians need to endure and the benefits that come as a result. 1 Pet. 3:18 states:

> **For Christ also hath once suffered for sins, the just for the unjust, that he might bring us to God, being put to death in the flesh, but quickened by the Spirit."** Concerning us, 1 Pet. 4:1 states, **"Forasmuch then as Christ hath suffered for us in the flesh, arm yourselves likewise with the same mind: for he that hath suffered in the flesh hath ceased from sin.**

Christ was put to death in the flesh through the suffering for sins, which He endured on the cross. This is important for each of us to understand, as we also are to be partakers of His sufferings (1 Peter. 4:13). It takes a true commitment to Christ to really suffer for Him, especially since this suffering is what causes us to die to ourselves (as Christ died on the cross), and cease from sin. To die to oneself and live for Christ is a commitment that few are willing to make.

Most of us are committed to live this life for ourselves, and serve the Lord as it fits into our schedules. God's Word instructs us that whatsoever we do in word or deed, we are to do all in the name of the Lord Jesus (Col. 3:17). We are to do all things heartily, as unto the Lord, and not unto men: for our lives are to be lived to serve Jesus Christ (Col. 3:23-24). We are to present our bodies as living sacrifices unto God, which is our reasonable service. We are no longer to be conformed to this world, but we are to be transformed by the renewing of our minds to prove the good, acceptable, and perfect will of God (Rom. 12:12). Many refuse to make this commitment because they really believe that God is asking too much of them, and fail to see the great benefits that make it worth doing. How sad for us! Jesus stated in Matthew 16:24-27:

> **If any man will come after me, let him deny himself, and take up his cross, and follow me. For whosoever will save his life shall lose it, and whosoever will lose his life for my sake shall find it. For what is a man profited, if he shall gain the whole world, and lose his own soul? or what shall a man give in exchange for his soul? For the Son of man shall come in the glory of his Father with his angels; and then he shall reward every man according to his works.**

God never asks us to give up anything without having something better for us. Mk. 10:29-30 states:

> **Verily I say unto you, there is no man that hath left house, or brethren, or sisters, or father, or mother, or wife, or children, or lands, for my sake, and the gospel's, But he shall receive an hundredfold now IN THIS TIME, houses, and brethren, and sisters, and mothers, and children, and lands, with persecutions; and in the world to came eternal life.** (capitals added).

Examples of Committed Lives

God's Word is filled with examples of men who have lived committed lives to serve Him. Let's look at a few that are recorded in the book of Daniel. The book of Daniel begins by speaking of the captives that were carried out of Judah by Nebuchadnezzar king of Babylon. These captives were taken during the reign of Jehoiakim king of Judah. Among these were Daniel, Hananiah, Mishael and Azariah. The last three are better known as Shadrach, Meshach and Abednego, the names given to them by the prince of the eunuchs in Babylon.

These were four of the captives who were selected to be taught and learn the tongue of the Chaldeans (Babylonians). However, Daniel purposed in his heart not to defile himself with the portion of the king of Babylon's meat, nor of the wine, which he drank. He therefore convinced the prince of the eunuchs to prove them for ten days, during which time they would eat pulse (seeds, vegetables, beans, and lentils) and drink water. At the end of the ten days their countenances appeared fairer and fatter in flesh than those, which ate the portion of the king's meat. This would have most likely also included other captives from Judah.

As a result of the commitment that these four men had to God in not defiling themselves with that which was contrary to His law, God gave them knowledge and skill in learning and wisdom that far exceeded the rest. When they stood before the king of Babylon after three years, they were found ten times better than all the magicians and astrologers of Babylon (Daniel chapter one).

Each of these four men also experienced a great deliverance from God because of their commitment to Him. When King Nebuchadnezzar made a sixty cubit image of gold and commanded all people, nations, and languages to fall down and worship it: Shadrach, Meshach, and Abednego refused. They refused being fully aware that the punishment for not doing so was to be cast into a burning fiery furnace. Upon their last chance to fall down and worship the image before being cast into the furnace, they responded by saying:

> **O Nebuchadnezzar, we are not careful to answer thee in this matter. If it be so, our God whom we serve is able to deliver us from the burning fiery furnace, and he will deliver us out of thine hand, O king, But if not, be it known unto thee, O king, that we will not serve thy gods, nor worship the golden image which thou hast set up** (Dan. 3:16-18).

Notice the true commitment that these men had to serving God. For these men, to fall down and worship the idol was not an option. There was only one answer they could give to the king. They knew God had the ability to deliver them, BUT IF NOT, that was irrelevant. They were bound (committed) to their course of action regardless of the circumstances.

This is the kind of commitment that is pleasing to God. Their commitment was not based upon what God could, should, or would do for them. They were committed to serve God whether He delivered them or not. They were cast into the fiery furnace, and that is where God met and delivered them. As a result they received freedom to worship God and were promoted in the province of Babylon (Dan. 3:1-30).

We should believe and expect God to perform His Word in our lives (and He will), but our commitment to Him cannot be based upon what we want from Him. If it is, we will probably find that it is not really genuine. More often than not, the circumstances and appearance of things seem to be contrary to God's Word, and promises, that are to be brought forth in our lives. This causes many to compromise, turn back, or look to other options. It is only those who are really committed that have the ability to stand fast regardless of the way things may appear to be.

After the Medes and Persians defeated Babylon, Daniel was set in a position of great authority by Darius the Mede. This caused the other presidents and princes to be envious, and they sought to find an occasion to trap him. Being able to find no fault in him, they devised a plan to use his faithful commitment to God against him. They established a decree and craftily got King Darius to sign it. In this decree no man was to make any petition of any God or man, except for King Darius, for thirty days. Anyone in violation was to be cast into the den of lions.

Even after Daniel KNEW it had been signed, he went to his house and opened his windows toward Jerusalem, kneeled down and prayed three times a day, doing just as he did before. To hide what he was doing, or cease to pray for thirty days was not an option for Daniel. He was committed to it.

Although the king was sorry he signed the decree, Daniel was still cast into the den of lions. However, God shut the lion's mouths and they did him no harm. The next morning Daniel was taken out of the den, and those that accused him were cast in and devoured (Daniel chapter 6).

As we can see, a true commitment to serve God does not necessarily mean that everything will run smoothly in our lives. At times, because of our commitment, just the opposite can be true. However, nothing can be compared to the end results of a faithful commitment to truly serve God.

Chapter 8

STEADFAST

The words that are translated in the bible as steadfast mean to be unmovable, stable, solid, firm, established, sure and settled. When someone is truly steadfast it means that they cannot be moved by any circumstance or event. This is how the bible instructs each of us to be concerning our walk with God. For anyone to be this steadfast, everything that causes *any* instability must be removed. Job 11:13-15 states:

> **If thou prepare thine heart, and stretch out thine hands toward him; If iniquity be in thine hand, put it far away, and let not wickedness dwell in thy tabernacles. For then shalt thou lift up thy face without spot; yea, thou shalt be stedfast, and shalt not fear.**

Everything we know to be sin must be put far from us, and we must strive to live an obedient life to God's Word. Psalm 78:5-10 & 37 states:

> **For he established a testimony in Jacob, and appointed a new law in Israel, which he commanded our fathers, that they should make them known to their children:**

> That the generation to come might know them, even the children which should be born; who should arise and declare them to their children: That they might set their hope in God, and not forget the works of God, but keep his commandments: and might not be as their fathers, a stubborn and rebellious generation; a generation that set not their heart aright, and whose spirit was not stedfast with God. The children of Ephraim, being armed, and carrying bows, turned back in the day of battle. They kept not the covenant of God, and refused to walk in his law. (vs. 37) For their heart was not right with him, neither were they stedfast in his covenant.

It is through learning and obeying God's Word that we prepare and set our hearts right, and make our spirits steadfast with God. Any part of God's Word that is disobeyed is the same as refusing to walk in His covenant. More than anything else, this is the main reason why so many turns back in the spiritual battles we face every day. We want to take part of God's Word, but reject or ignore the parts we do not like, or are just simply unwilling to follow. This will not allow for a steadfast Christian life.

The Steadfastness of the First Century Church

We find an excellent example for us to follow recorded in the book of Acts during the first days of the church. The first converts of the New Testament church continued steadfastly in God's Word, fellowship, breaking of bread, and in prayers (Acts 2:41-42). They did not just have one or two days set aside to worship God, but continued daily in these activities (Acts 2:46). This is a key to become steadfast with God. Many of us just want to take one day a week to set apart for God, but then do little to nothing spiritually for the next six. We need to become more aware of what God has done for us in Christ, and give more of ourselves to the work of the Lord. 1 Cor. 15:57-58 states:

> **But thanks be to God, which giveth us the victory through our Lord Jesus Christ. Therefore, my beloved brethren, be ye stedfast, unmoveable, always abounding in the work of the Lord, forasmuch as ye know that your labour is not in vain in the Lord.**

To many of us labor for the things that pertain to this life, but neglect to labor in the work of the Lord that will profit us eternally.

Of course many of us have responsibilities in this life that is going to consume much of our time; but it is also necessary to make time to study, fellowship, and pray each and every day. It is greatly beneficial to devote as much our time, and ourselves, to God as possible. As we do we will find that God will give us plenty of time to take care of everything else, and all our needs will also be taken care of (Matt. 6:33).

Steadfastness comes by being Rooted and Built Up in Christ

The book of Colossians also gives us some excellent insight into this subject of being steadfast. Col. 2:5-7 states:

> **For though I be absent in the flesh, yet am I with you in the spirit, joying and beholding your order, and the stedfastness of your faith in Christ. As ye have therefore received Christ Jesus the Lord, so walk ye in him: Rooted and built up in him, and stablished in the faith, as ye have been taught, abounding therein with thanksgiving.**

Remember, to be steadfast is to be unmovable, stable, firm, etc. The bible often compares believers as trees because we are to bear fruit, and to teach us what it truly is to be rooted and built up in Christ. A tree is an excellent example of something that is unmovable, stable, solid, firm, established, sure and settled. For example, let's consider a palm tree, which is a common tree in Israel, and could very well be what Paul had in mind when he wrote this passage of scripture. A palm tree often grows in sandy soil and has to endure severe wind and storms. Its roots grow deep into the soil until they find a rock and wrap themselves around it. Severe wind and storms can lay the tree over on its side, but cannot pull it up by the roots. After the storm it rises back up as it was before. We also need to be like a tree that is so rooted and grounded in Christ, our Rock, that none of life's storms can uproot us, or keep us down.

We are also to be built up in Christ as well. We will find that being rooted and built up coincide together. It is interesting to know that the root of a tree often goes as deep, sometimes deeper, in the ground as the tree is tall. The taller the tree the deeper the roots must go into the ground to stabilize the tree. What is seen of a skyscraper is also only a part of the building. It is also build down into the ground as a means of stability. Otherwise strong winds and storms would cause the building to topple.

Things Seen and Unseen

When we look at a tree or skyscraper we can actually only see a part of it, because up to half of it is in the ground. This also gives us an illustration of our Christian life, and what makes us steadfast. Our life consists of things that are seen, and of things that are not seen. The things that are not seen are what we do that is just between God and ourselves. These are the things that cause us to be rooted in Christ. Think about it! What do you do when you are alone and no one is watching? Do you pray and study God's Word or involve yourself with fleshly, worldly, or even sinful activities. The part of our Christian life that is not seen by others is what truly reveals just how rooted and steadfast we are. We can appear to be built up by what others see from the outside for a time, but those who are not rooted will fall during trials and tribulations. Phil. 1:27 states:

> **Only let your conversation be as it becometh the gospel of Christ: that whether I come and see you, or else be absent, I may hear of your affairs, that ye stand fast in one spirit, with one mind striving together for the faith of the gospel.**

The most important thing to remember is that God is always present and sees the steadfastness of our faith. To be steadfast in faith is also essential to be able to resist the devil, and walk in victory over the afflictions that each of us face in this world. 1 Peter 5: 8-9 states:

> **Be sober, be vigilant; because your adversary the devil, as a roaring lion, walketh about, seeking whom he may devour: Whom resist stedfast in the faith, knowing that the same afflictions are accomplished in your brethren that are in the world.**

Just how steadfast we are is something that we need to take very seriously. We learn from the book of Hebrews that we, the true believers, are Christ's house IF we hold fast the confidence and the rejoicing of our hope FIRM to the end. We are warned not to be like those of Israel who should have been steadfast, but hardened their hearts in the wilderness. We are instructed to make sure there is no evil heart of unbelief in us, which would cause us to depart from God; or that we become hardened through the DECEITFULNESS of sin. **"For we are made partakers of Christ, if we hold the beginning of our confidence stedfast unto the end"** (Heb. 3:6-14).

We are warned about all these things because they are real threats in our lives as children of God. Even when we are walking steadfast with God, we should always keep on our guard and remember the words of 2 Peter 3:17, **"Ye therefore, beloved, seeing ye know these things before, beware lest ye also, being led away with the error of the wicked, fall from your own stedfastness."**

Chapter 9

SEEKING GOD

What is it to truly seek God? Why is it necessary? Just how important is it in our lives? Although the answers to these questions seem to be obvious, many still fall far short of seeking God as we are instructed to in His Word. The Hebrew and Greek words (baqash, zeteo) that are translated as 'seek' in the bible mean: to follow (for pursuit or search), to worship, to search out, investigate, and to endeavor.

The scriptures instruct us to seek God because He must be found. Isa. 45:15 states, **"Verily thou art a God that hidest thyself, O God of Israel, the Saviour."** One only seeks something that is lost or hidden, and because it is desperately wanted. We lost our relationship with God because of sin and He has therefore hidden Himself from us. Hos. 5:15 states, **"I will go and return to my place, till they acknowledge their offence, and seek my face: in their affliction they will seek me early."**

To truly find God is not something that is out of our reach or something that we can just take for grant. As the word seek implies, it requires an endeavoring search and pursuit for Him. Jer. 29:13-14a states, **"And ye shall seek me, and find me, when ye shall search for me with all your heart. And I will be found of you, saith the LORD"** (see also Deut.

4:29). For someone to seek God with all their heart is actually a very rare thing considering it is essential in order to truly find Him.

To seek God with all of one's heart is to put this endeavoring search and pursuit for Him above all else. It must become the most important thing in one's life.

Sadly to say, many of God's people never really find Him apart from their salvation. Few find that intimate personal relationship with Him that is available to His people. Many even speak of God as if He is far away or a stranger to them.

We will find that when our needs are not being met in any area of our lives, and God does not seem to be present, it is a result of our failure to seek Him. Ps. 34:10 states:

> **The young lions do lack, and suffer hunger: but they that seek the Lord shall not want any good thing.** Heb. 11:6 also states, **But without faith it is impossible to please him: for he that cometh to God must believe that he is, and that he is a rewarder of them that diligently seek him.**

The scriptures teach that victory, deliverance, prosperity, understanding, and even life itself are all benefits of seeking God (Ps. 34:4, 2 Chr. 31:21, Pro. 28:5, Amos 5:6).

Outstanding Examples from the Old Testament Kings

A study of the kings of Judah gives some valuable insight into the importance of truly seeking God. Upon salvation we are made kings and priests unto our God (Rev. 1:5-6). What is written about the kings of Israel and Judah instructs us, as kings, how we are to live and reign upon the earth. When speaking of the kings of Judah, God's Word records whether or not they did that which was good and right in the eyes of the Lord, and to what extent each one sought God. Let's take a look at a few of these kings.

King Rehoboam's Compromising Reign

Solomon's son, Rehoboam, was the first king to reign over Judah after the nation was divided into two kingdoms. He began his reign walking in obedience to God's Word, but soon forsook the law of the Lord, and took the nation with him. Because of their transgression, God sent Shishak the king of the Egyptians against them. He was therefore able to conquer the fenced cities of Judah. As a result, Rehoboam and the people of Judah humbled themselves before God (2 Chr. 11:17, 12:1-6). 2 Chr. 12:7-8 then states:

> **And when the LORD saw that they humbled themselves, the word of the LORD came to Shemaiah, saying, They have humbled themselves; therefore I will not destroy them, but I will grant them some deliverance; and my wrath shall not be poured out upon Jerusalem by the hand of Shishak. Nevertheless they shall be his servants; that they may know my service, and the service of the kingdoms of the countries.**

Take notice that God did not fully deliver them, but only granted them some deliverance and left them as servants. Why didn't God grant them a complete deliverance? The answer is found in verse 14, which states, **"And he did evil, because he prepared not his heart to seek the LORD"**. Rehoboam humbled himself because of the affliction, but never sought God with all his heart.

The majority of those in the church today can easily be compared to King Rehoboam. We start our walk zealous for God, but soon lose that zeal and forsake His Word. We become unwilling to fully take up our cross, deny ourselves, and follow Christ. God's chastening causes us to humble ourselves, but being yet unwilling to give up the things of this life (the cares of the world), we never prepare our hearts to really seek after Him. As a result, we find ourselves continually falling into sin, doing evil, and never enter into an intimate relationship with God. We are in desperate need of deliverances that will never fully come without diligently seeking God, yet we do not diligently seek Him because we do not want or desire Him nearly enough. God remains hidden in the lives of many believers along with all that He is and has to offer.

King Asa's Great Beginning

King Asa gives us a much better example of what we need to do to seek God, and how we are to do it. He is introduced as a king that did that which was good and right in the eyes of the Lord his God. He began his reign by removing from Judah everything that did not pertain to the worship of the God of Israel. He took away the altars of the strange gods, the high places, broke down the images, and cut down the groves. He then commanded Judah to seek the God of Israel (2 Chr. 14:1-5). This is an excellent example of what we must do spiritually. In order for anyone to seek God with all their heart and soul, they must remove everything from their life that does not pertain to the worship of God. When anyone seriously searches for something they remove everything that is in their way, or blocks their view.

Each thing that the Word tells us that Asa removed from Judah is also things we need to remove from our own lives. Before salvation we all walked according to the course of this world, according to the prince of the power of the air (Satan). Our lifestyle was in the lusts of the flesh, and we worshipped the things (gods) of this world (Eph. 2:2-3). Each of the gods spoken of in the Old Testament reflects the things that are worshipped in the world. For examples, there were gods (idols) made of silver and gold as they have always been worshipped for their value. There were male and female fertility gods as sex is worshipped in almost every culture throughout the world.

Even more important, the worship of strange gods is strictly forbidden in both covenants because there is a demonic reality behind them. God instructed Israel to bring their offerings unto Him, unto the door of the tabernacle, that they would no more offer their sacrifices to devils (Lev. 17:3-7). The Apostle Paul stated that the things, which the Gentiles sacrifice, they sacrifice to devils of which we are not to have fellowship. We cannot drink and be partakers of both the cup and table of the Lord, and the cup and table of devils (1 Cor. 10:20-21).

The high places, images, and groves were also removed. The groves are usually in reference to the goddess Asherah, the foremost fertility deity of the Canaanites. The high places and groves were places of worship. The high places were usually located on a mountain or hill top where there was an altar, and often a sanctuary and image. Many of the kings would remove the altars and images, but leave the high places. This left a foothold for the worship of strange gods to enter back into the nation. Many of us are held in bondage to immorality because we have not removed our high places. We continue to go to questionable places, watch 'R' or 'X' rated movies, listen to worldly music (all music is a form of worship), look at immoral magazines, and read ungodly books. Most Christians today view many of these things as harmless, and believe that they have little to no effect on them spiritually. Nothing could be farther from the truth. All of these things keep us carnal and lukewarm, and put images (that we are to remove) in our minds that capture our imaginations. 2 Cor. 10:4-5 states:

> **(For the weapons of our warfare are not carnal, but mighty through God to the pulling down of strong holds;) Casting down imaginations, and every high thing that exalteth itself against the knowledge of God, and bringing into captivity every thought to the obedience of Christ.**

It is also surprising that many Christians unknowingly dabble in some sort of magic, sorcery, or witchcraft. These may include horoscopes, psychics, Ouija boards, various card games, and even the use of certain drugs. The Greek word for witchcraft is 'pharmakeia', which means: medication (pharmacy), magic and sorcery. It is taken from the word 'pharmakeus', which means: a drug, spell giving potion, a druggist (pharmacist), poisoner, magician or sorcerer. Doing any kind of mind-altering drug is a form of witchcraft. All such things need to be removed from our lives if we are going to truly seek God.

God gave King Asa a time of rest as a result of seeking Him. During this time of rest Asa fortified the cities of Judah and built up his army. When an attack from the enemy did come Asa was prepared, cried unto the Lord and received a great deliverance (2 Chr. 14:6-15).

This is another excellent example for us to follow. It is easy to get complacent when everything is going smoothly in our lives. We have the tendency to pray and study less, and just get spiritually slothful. Then when the attack of the enemy does come we are weak, unprepared, and suffer defeat. We need to use times of rest to build up and fortify ourselves against a spiritual attack that will eventually come. We do this by staying diligent in seeking God through prayer, study, fasting and fellowshipping with others. Although God gives us needed times of rest, no Christian is not going to experience the spiritual warfare that we are all called unto.

After God gave Asa this great deliverance, He then sent him a message, saying:

> **Hear ye me, Asa, and all Judah and Benjamin; The LORD is with you, while ye be with him; and if ye seek him, he will be found of you; but if ye forsake him, he will forsake you. Now for a long season Israel hath been without the true God, and without a teaching priest, and without law. But when they in their trouble did turn unto the LORD God of Israel, and sought him, he was found of them** (2 Chr. 15:2-4).

Regrettably, times of trouble are needed in our lives to cause us to seek God. More often than not, those who really seek God do so during a great time of trouble or hardship.

Asa then gathered the people together to enter into a covenant to seek the Lord God with all their heart and soul. Those who would not were to be put to death (2 Chr. 15:8-14). Verse 15 then states:

> **And all Judah rejoiced at the oath: for they had sworn with all their heart, and sought him with their whole desire; and he was found of them: and the LORD gave them rest round about.**

In order to seek God with all our hearts we must desire Him above all else.

Another important thing we learn from King Asa is that one cannot get so strong that he cannot fall (see 1 Cor. 10:12). Years later, Asa experienced another attack from the enemy, but reacted in a completely different way. Rather than relying on God to deliver them, he hired the king of Syria, using the silver and gold out of the treasures of the house of the Lord. It worked, but God was not pleased. He sent a prophet to rebuke him, whom Asa put in prison. At the end of Asa's reign he was greatly diseased in his feet. This could reveal that his once strong walk with God had deteriorated over the years. Seeking God must become a part of our everyday lifestyle. 1 Chr. 16:11 states, **"Seek the LORD and his strength, seek his face continually."** Asa must have fallen short of this toward the end of his reign.

King Jehoshaphat's Good Reign

King Jehoshaphat is another good example for us to look at. The Word states that God was with Jehoshaphat because he sought the Lord God of his fathers. God therefore established the kingdom in his hand, and he had riches and honor in abundance (2 Chr. 17:1-6).

However, as no one is without fault, Jehoshaphat later joined forces with Ahab; a wicked ungodly king that reigned over Israel. This unequally yoked them together and brought God's wrath against Jehoshaphat (see 2 Chr. 18-19:2). Even though they lost the battle because of God's wrath, Jehoshaphat received God's grace and mercy and was himself delivered from the battle. The Word then states, **"Nevertheless there are good things found in thee, in that thou hast taken away the groves out of the land, and hast prepared thine heart to seek God"** (2 Chr. 19:3). Remember, Rehoboam did evil because he did not prepare his heart to seek God. Good things were found in Jehoshaphat because he did.

Jehoshaphat also later received full and complete deliverance in a war that followed against the Ammonites, Moabites, and Edomites. When this great multitude came against him, the Word states:

> **And Jehoshaphat feared, and set himself to seek the LORD, and proclaimed a fast throughout all Judah. And Judah gathered themselves together, to ask help of the LORD: even out of all the cities of Judah they came to seek the LORD** (2 Chr. 20:3-4).

As a result of Judah seeking Him in fasting and prayer God claimed this battle as His own, saying:

> **Be not afraid nor be dismayed by reason of this multitude; for the battle is not yours, but God's. Tomorrow go ye down against them: ye shall not need to fight in this battle: set yourselves, stand ye still, and see the salvation of the LORD with you, O Judah and Jerusalem: fear not, nor be dismayed; tomorrow go out against them: for the LORD will be with you** (2 Chr. 20: 15-17).

Take notice that God made it clear that they would not need to fight in this battle, but they still had to go out against them. They were required to be on the battlefield. This is also the duty of every Christian. We often do not receive God's deliverances in our lives because we expect God to fight for us without us going out against the enemy, or even being on the battlefield. We are workers together with God and need to be present at all times (2 Cor. 6:1-2).

In this battle, when the people began to sing and praise God, He destroyed the armies that had come out against them by turning each of the three armies against one another. God's people then took away an abundance of spoil that was found among the dead bodies of their enemies (2 Chr. 20). Seeking God is essential to walk in complete victory. It is only by SEEKING and FINDING God that we will see His salvation really manifested in our lives in such magnificent ways.

King Hezekiah and King Josiah

Just to briefly mention a couple more of Judah's kings, concerning King Hezekiah, 2 Chr. 31:20-21 states:

> **And thus did Hezekiah throughout all Judah, and wrought that which was good and right and truth before the LORD his God. And in every work that he began in the service of the house of God, and in the law, and in the commandments, to seek his God, he did it with all his heart, and prospered.**

King Josiah also did that which was good and right in the sight of God, and walked in the first ways of David his father, and declined neither to the right hand nor to the left. This is attributed to him seeking after God from the time he was young (2 Chr. 34:1-3).

The People Follow the King

All the kings of Judah came through the lineage of King David, whom God promised that the Messiah would come through his lineage and reign over Israel forever. His godly reign was set forth as an example for the other kings to follow. King David was the standard that all the other kings were measured against and compared too. It is interesting to observe, throughout scripture, that the people always followed the king. If the king sought God, so did the people. If the king turned away from God, so did the people. When Rehoboam (the first king of Judah after the nation was divided) forsook the law of the Lord, the people followed him. Jeroboam, the first king of Israel after the nation was divided, is continually spoken of as the man who made Israel to sin. This is because of the two golden calves he set up in Israel, which the people worshipped until God's judgment came against the nation to destroy it.

This leaves us without excuse. Our King is Jesus Christ. His life is set forth as the example that each of us are to follow (1 Pet. 2:21). He is the standard that each of us is to measure ourselves against and compare ourselves to. As the people always followed the king, those that are Christ's follow Him through His Spirit that dwells in each of us. It is instilled in each of us to follow Christ, our King, and seek God as He did.

Each of us just need to ask ourselves the questions: What do I want from my relationship with God? And even more important, just how much of God do I want (or need) in my life? The answer you give yourself to these questions will determine to what extent you will be willing to seek God. If we give God our all, there is no limit to what He will do for us. If we give Him a little, we should not really expect to receive great things from Him. We can be like Rehoboam, and get some deliverance, or like many of the other kings who received complete deliverances, great victories, and lived prosperous godly lives.

Chapter 10

FAITHFULNESS

A faithful person is one who is trustworthy, sure, true, reliable, devoted, steadfast, and consistent. Many Christians fall far short of being faithful to God in living a true Christian life. Many are not faithful to keep or study God's Word, pray, tithe, or give to those in need. Those who continually fall into sin do so because of their unfaithfulness.

There are great rewards for being faithful. A faithful man will be preserved by the Lord (Ps. 31:23), put in positions of trust and authority (Lk. 12:42-44), receive from the mouth of the Lord (Num. 12:7-8), and be highly esteemed in His eyes (Ps 101:6).

Nehemiah put those who were faithful in charge of Jerusalem and made them treasurers (Neh. 7:12, 13:13). Those who sought an accusation against Daniel could not find any error or fault in him because he was faithful (Dan. 6:4). As these men show, those who do have a faithful walk can clearly be seen as a result.

There is also a great loss of rewards, privileges, and position for unfaithfulness in any area of our Christian walk (1 Sam. 2:22-35). Our faithfulness in this life is what will determine our eternal position and rewards in the life to come (2 Cor. 5:10). Each of us will only live this life one time. It is more important than most of us realize. Once it's over we do not get a second chance, so we need to make the most of each and every day.

Each one of us is a steward of everything that God gives us in this life. Our stewardship can include the gospel (1 Cor. 4:1) as well as any earthly possessions. This life is our proving ground. The bible says that it is required of a steward that he is found faithful (1 Cor. 4:2). Each of us is to faithfully serve Christ. The bible gives clear warning to remain faithful until the coming of the Lord, as we do not know the day or hour of His return. Those who are found faithful at His coming will be made rulers over His household. Those who are not will suffer terrible consequences (Matt. 24:42-51, Lk. 12:42-48).

Jesus Taught Many Parables on Faithfulness

Jesus gave a parable of a man travelling into a far country, which called his servants, and delivered unto them his goods. He gave one man five talents, another two, and to another one. He distributed to them according to the ability of each man. The one who received the five talents and the one who received the two talents both traded with them, and doubled what they had received. The other man hid his lord's money in the ground. Upon their lord's return, he said unto the two who had doubled what was delivered unto them, **"Well done, thou good and faithful servant: thou hast been faithful, over a few things, I will make thee ruler over many things: enter thou into the joy of the lord."** He called the other a wicked and slothful servant. He told him that he should have at the least put the money to the exchangers that he would have at least received it back with usury (interest). Concerning this man the Word states:

> **Take therefore the talent from him, and give it unto him that hath ten talents. For unto every one that hath shall be given, and he shall have abundance: but**

> **from him that hath not shall be taken away even that which he hath. And cast the unprofitable servant into outer darkness: there shall be weeping and gnashing of teeth** (Matt. 25:14-30).

The interpretation of this parable should be clear. The man travelling into a far country represents Christ, and we are the servants to which He has distributed His goods; each of us according to our ability. Notice that God is far more concerned about our faithfulness than our ability. Whatever we have, material or otherwise, has been given to us by Him. What we do with what Christ has given us in this life will determine our position in His kingdom.

There is a very similar parable recorded in the gospel of Luke (Lk. 19:11-27). In this parable Jesus speaks of a nobleman that went into a far country to receive a kingdom. He called his ten servants and delivered to each of them one pound, and said unto them, **"Occupy till I come."** After he received the kingdom, he returned and called his servants to find out how much each of them had gained by trading. The first had gained ten pounds. The nobleman responded by saying, **"Well, thou good servant: because thou hast been faithful in a very little, have thou authority over ten cities."** The second had gained five, and was given authority over five cities. One that did nothing with the pound had it taken from him and given to the one with ten pounds.

That which we receive in this lifetime is very little compared to what can be received in God's kingdom. Once again, we see that our faithfulness to the very little things in this life will determine our position and rewards in the next. The Word also states in Luke 16:10-11:

> **He that which is faithful in that which is least is faithful in that which is much: and he that is unjust in the least is unjust also in much. If therefore ye have not been faithful in the unrighteous mammon, who will commit to your trust the true riches.**

God's Word always proves itself to be true. A faithful person remains faithful (trustworthy) regardless of whether he is put in charge of very little or very much. Those who are not faithful to the little things of this life will have proven themselves not be faithful in the true riches of the next.

Chapter 11

SEPARATION

Separation is not only one of the most important biblical principles, but it is also one of the most neglected. Few Christians today live the separated lives that we are instructed to in God's Word. Contrary to innumerable scriptures, it is surprising to realize just how many of God's people do not even believe that we are to live separated lives. It is often a very touchy subject matter. Many do not want to live a separated life, others do not see the need, and yet others do not understand how we can be a separated people and still be a witness and preach the gospel to the people of the world. God's Word does instruct us to do both, and therefore reveals how we can live separated lives and still be effective ministers of the gospel.

God Uses Our Separation as a Witnessing Tool

Contrary to the way many believe, living a separated life is one of the most powerful witnessing tools that we have at our disposal. Scripture teaches that we are ambassadors for Christ (2 Cor. 5:20). As ambassadors we are to speak for the kingdom of heaven, and show the inhabitants of the earth their standing and relationship with God. Isa. 59:2 states, **"But your iniquities have separated between you and your God, and your sins have hid his face from you, that he will not**

hear." This scripture reveals the spiritual state and condition of every unsaved person. When we refuse to live separate lives from the people of the world we are actually giving them the message that they are not separated from God by their iniquities, and their sins have not hid His face from them. As ambassadors, our relationship with the people of the world should reflect their relationship with God. Although this will bring persecution to our lives, it will also cause many to examine their lives and seek a right relationship with God. It will actually open the door to preach the gospel to those who are ready to receive it.

Separation is a Biblical Concept Throughout Scripture

Separation is a biblical concept throughout both the Old and New Testaments. Many have the false understanding that the Old Testament scriptures have little or nothing to do with the church, not considering that many of the Old Testament scriptures are quoted in the New Testament. This means that they apply just as much to the church as they did to the nation of Israel. There are literally hundreds of Old Testament passages of scripture quoted in the New Testament. Every time we see the words, "it is written", it is a quote taken from the Old Testament. Even though we are not under the Old Covenant, biblical principles remain the same. God has always commanded His people to be separated from the people of the world, and for some very important reasons. God knows that if His people are not separate from the people of the world, they will be corrupted by them. Evil communications does corrupt good manners (1 Cor. 15:33).

Israel Called to be a Separated People

Let's look at some examples. The making of the nation of Israel began with the call of Abram (Abraham). Gen. 12:1 states, **"Now the LORD had said unto Abram, Get thee out of thy country, and from thy kindred, and from thy father's house, unto a land that I will shew thee."** God instructed Abram to GET OUT of his country (where he served other gods, Joshua 24:2-3), to leave his kindred, his father's house, and go unto a land that God would show him. This was the land of Canaan, which the bible speaks of as a land that flowed with milk and honey (Ex. 13:5, 33:3). It was a land that was different from all other lands. It was a land that God cared for, and His eyes were always upon (Deut. 11:10-12). It was a land that would abundantly supply all their needs.

What God instructed Abram to do is a natural example of what takes place in our lives upon salvation. The land of Canaan was a type of God's kingdom that we receive upon being born again (Jn. 3:5). Upon salvation we are delivered from the power of darkness and translated (removed from one place and placed in another) into the kingdom of God's dear Son (Col. 1:13). Born again believers begin their lives in God's kingdom at the moment of salvation. We are chosen and called out of the world, and are therefore no longer of the world (Jn. 15:19). We are born from (of) God (from above) and are now citizens of heaven (Phil. 3:20); no longer to live our lives according to this world. Upon salvation we leave our country, (which is the world,) our kindred, and our father's house as we are born into the family of God. Living our lives in obedience to God's Word might even cause the need for us to separate ourselves from unsaved members of our natural family. Jesus stated:

> **Think not that I am come to send peace on earth: I came not to send peace, but a sword. For I am come to set a man at variance against his father, and the daughter against her mother, and the daughter in law against her mother in law. And a man's foes shall be they of his own household** (Matt. 10:34-36).

As we are no longer of the world, we are no longer to love the world, or the things of the world. As the world and all that is in it is not of God, we are to separate ourselves from it (1 Jn. 2:15-17). This actually puts us at enmity with the world and causes us to be hated and persecuted by the world (Jn. 15:18-20). Scripture states that all that will live godly in

Christ Jesus shall suffer persecution (2 Tim. 3:12). If we are not suffering persecution we are not living the godly lives that we are called unto.

God has done everything necessary to make sure His people are a separated people. Abraham, Isaac, and Jacob had clear instruction not to mingle with the people of the land. However, at one point Jacob seemed willing to mingle with the Canaanite people over an incident where a prince of the Hivites, descendants of Canaan, defiled his daughter Dinah. The two sides communed about making marriages with each other, and thereby becoming ONE PEOPLE (See Genesis 34). God's sovereign plan did not permit this to take place.

Shortly afterward, Israel ended up in Egypt as a result of a famine that God brought upon the land (Gen. 41:25, 28, 32). This was to insure that they would remain a separated people. In Egypt, the Hebrew shepherds were an abomination to the Egyptians, so they could not dwell among them; but dwelt in an apparently uninhabited part of Egypt known as Goshen (Gen. 46:34). It was there, removed from the danger of mixing with other people, that Israel grew into a great nation.

Upon being delivered from the bondage of Egypt, God commanded them to drive out all the inhabitants of the land of Canaan that they were to receive as their inheritance. Ex. 23:31-33 states:

> **And I will set thy bounds from the Red sea even unto the sea of the Philistines, and from the desert unto the river; for I will deliver the inhabitants of the land into your hand; and thou shalt drive them out before thee. Thou shalt make no covenant with them, nor with their gods. They shall not dwell in thy land, lest they make thee sin against me: for if thou serve their gods, it will surely be a snare unto thee.**

Israel had clear instruction not to let the Canaanites dwell in the land with them. This was to prevent them from sinning against God by serving their idol gods. Num. 33:51-53 also states:

> Speak unto the children of Israel, and say unto them, When ye are passed over Jordan into the land of Canaan; Then ye shall drive out all the inhabitants of the land from before you, and destroy all their pictures, and destroy all their molten images, and quite pluck down all their high places: And ye shall dispossess the inhabitants of the land, and dwell therein: for I have given you the land to possess it.

Once they entered into the land of their inheritance, they were no longer to live as they did in Egypt, or the way of the Canaanites who then inhabited the land. Lev. 18:2-3 states,

> Speak unto the children of Israel, and say unto them, I am the LORD your God. After the doings of the land of Egypt, wherein ye dwelt, shall ye not do: and after the doings of the land of Canaan, whither I bring you, shall ye not do: neither shall ye walk in their ordinances.

Throughout the bible, Egypt is a type of the world system. The Canaanites were a cursed race of people (Gen. 9:25), and are therefore a type of our carnal nature that we are to put to death through God's Spirit (Rom. 8:13). As we are translated into the kingdom of God upon salvation, the same principle holds true with us. We are no longer to live our lives as we did before. We are no longer to walk after the course of this world or have our lifestyle in the lusts of our flesh (Eph. 2:2-3). This will seem strange and bring persecution from those of the world who we previously associated with (1 Pet. 4:2-4).

The rest of Leviticus chapters 18, 19, and 20 list the abominable practices of the Canaanite people, and strictly forbid those of Israel to commit any such acts. Lev. 20:22-26 then states:

> **Ye shall therefore keep all my statutes, and all my judgments, and do them: that the land, whither I bring you to dwell therein, spue you not out. And ye shall not walk in the manners of the nation, which I cast out before you: for they committed all these things, and therefore I abhorred them. But I have said unto you, Ye shall inherit their land, and I will give it unto you to possess it, a land that floweth with milk and honey: I am the LORD your God, which have separated you from other people. Ye shall therefore put difference between clean beasts and unclean, and between unclean fowls and clean: and ye shall not make your souls abominable by beasts, or by fowl, or by any manner of living thing that creepeth on the ground, which I have separated from you as unclean. And ye shall be holy unto me: for I the LORD am holy, and have severed you from other people that ye should be mine.**

God stated previously that the land itself had spewed (vomited) out the Canaanite inhabitants because of their abominations (Lev. 18:25, 28). It was actually because of their abominable lifestyle that God abhorred them. Israel was given clear warning that the same fate could also happen to them if they did not keep and do God's statutes and judgments. As the land is a type of God's kingdom, these abominations are not tolerated in God's kingdom either. The Kingdom itself would spew out all those who commit such acts.

We also see that God Himself separated Israel from all other people. He called them out of the world shown by their deliverance from Egypt. He gave them a land where they were to drive out all who dwelt there, and commanded them not to seek the peace or prosperity of the other nations (Deut. 23:6). They were to be holy (set apart) as God is holy. This was made possible by God severing them from other people to make them His own. The word 'sever' means to tear away by force.

We also see from this passage of scripture that because God had separated Israel from other people, they were to put a difference between clean and unclean beasts and fowls. The unclean beasts were therefore a type of the Gentile nations (people). This is also seen in Acts chapter ten where God gave Peter a vision of unclean animals on a sheet let down from heaven, saying, **"Rise Peter, kill and eat"**. This vision was to prepare Peter to preach the gospel to the Gentiles who were previously unclean, as they were not in covenant with God, and their sins were not atoned for.

There is a powerful spiritual message behind this. God's Word is the spiritual man's food. It is what produces salvation, faith, growth, and strength in His people. As Israel was not to eat of the beasts and fowls which God had separated from them as unclean, we are not to eat of the filthy communication (lifestyles) of the people of the world, which He has separated from us as unclean. There are many in the body of Christ who are very concerned about what kinds of natural foods they eat, (which we should be,) but make their souls abominable by feeding their spirits from the filthiness of the world. We watch all kinds of immorality on T.V., carry on all kinds of ungodly conversations, and live our lives much like the people of the world. We have not received the most important message of all.

God was very well aware that if Israel lived among the Canaanite people, they would eventually serve their gods and walk after their manners. He continually warned them that if they did not drive out all the inhabitants from the land, those that remained would be pricks in their eyes, thorns in their sides, and would vex them in the land where they dwelt (Num. 33:55). We know from scripture that Israel did not drive out all the inhabitants of the land, and they did end up serving the gods of Canaan and of the nations around them (see the book of Judges). Refusing to live a separated life is the number one reason why they continually fell into sin and worshipped other gods. This took place until they were cast out of the land of their inheritance (Joshua.

23:12-13). When they did not drive out all the inhabitants of the land, they set themselves up for failure, and were doomed from the start.

The Church Called to be a Separated People

As biblical principles remain the same, those of the church are just as much at risk as was those of Israel. God therefore severs (separates) each member of the church from the world upon salvation by translating him or her into His kingdom. As God has done His part, we must also do ours. The church is therefore also commanded to be a separated people as was the nation of Israel. We are not to be partakers with them that live ungodly lifestyles (Eph. 5:3-7). We are to have no fellowship with the unfruitful works of darkness, but rather reprove them (Eph. 5:11). Any ungodly relationships we refuse to remove from our lives blurs our spiritual vision (pricks in our eyes), and causes difficulty in our walk with God (thorns in our sides). These ungodly relationships cause us to compromise our walk because of the pressure to live as those of the world. Our lack of separation is also one of the main reasons we continually fall into sin, and live our lives much like the people of the world.

One of the most well-known New Testament passages of scripture concerning separation is found in 2 Corinthians 6:14-18, which states:

> **Be ye not unequally yoked together with unbelievers: for what fellowship hath righteousness with unrighteousness? and what communion hath light with darkness? And what concord hath Christ with belial? or what part hath he that believeth with an infidel? And what agreement hath the temple of God with idols? for ye are the temple of the living God; as God hath said, I will dwell in them, and walk in them; and I will be their God, and they shall be my people. Wherefore come out from among them, and be ye separate, saith the Lord, and touch not the unclean**

thing; and I will receive you, And will be a Father unto you, and ye shall be my sons and daughters, saith the Lord almighty.

This passage of scripture begins by instructing us not to be unequally yoked together with unbelievers. Scripture speaks of believers as clean and unbelievers as unclean. The natural example brought forth here is that a clean animal cannot be equally yoked together with an unclean animal. Clean animals, such as an ox, pull from their shoulders where the animals are yoked together. Unclean animals, such as a horse, pull from their chest. A harness is therefore used rather than a yoke. An unclean animal yoked to a clean animal would only put a great burden upon the clean animal. The clean animal would not only have to do all the labor, but would also have to contend (struggle) with the unclean animal at its side. This would cause the clean animal to quickly tire and grow weary.

This is exactly what takes place spiritually to those who remain unequally yoked together with unbelievers. They often complain that the Christian walk is hard. God's Word states that the way of the transgressor is hard (Pro. 13:15). Jesus stated that those who take His yoke upon them would find rest for their souls, for His yoke is easy, and his burden light (Matt. 11:28-30).

Therefore, as a clean and an unclean animal cannot really be yoked together, this scripture proceeds by asking five questions; with the answer to each being "NONE" (or no). Righteousness has no fellowship with unrighteousness, light has no communion with darkness, Christ has no concord with belial, he that believes has no part with an unbeliever, and the temple of God has no agreement with idols. All of these things are opposites and reveal the difference between believers and unbelievers. Believers are the temple of the living God, and need to separate themselves from all that is not like Him. Believers who do not live separate lives are unequally yoked with unbelievers.

1 Cor. 2:14 states, **"But the natural man receiveth not the things of the Spirit of God: for they are foolishness unto him: neither can he know them, because they are spiritually discerned"**. A natural man is in reference to an unsaved person. As an unsaved person has no ability to receive the things of God's Spirit, they have no ability to live in the kingdom of God with a believer. However, a believer is still wrapped up in this sinful body of flesh, and does have the ability to live in the world with an unbeliever. To put it simply, a believer must resort back to the world, and walk after the flesh, in order to have any kind of a relationship with an unbeliever. If not separated from the people of the world we will (to some extent) live our lives as they do.

God therefore instructs us to come out from among them, be separate, and touch not the unclean thing. Under the Old Covenant, the unclean thing was a dead body. Under the New Covenant, it would be those who are born dead in trespasses and sins (Eph. 2:1); those who are dead while they yet live (Matt. 8:22, 1 Tim. 5:6). Separation is essential for one to have a true relationship with God, as a Father has with his child (2 Cor. 6:14-18).

Separation in Marriage

With all this in mind, one of the most detrimental things a believer can do is to marry an unbeliever. Once again, we are warned about this throughout scripture. Deut. 7:3-4 states:

> **Neither shalt thou make marriages with them; thy daughter thou shalt not give unto his son, nor his daughter shalt thou, take unto thy son. For they will turn away thy son from following me, that they may serve other gods: so will the anger of the LORD be kindled against you, and destroy thee suddenly.**

Notice, God did not tell Israel that making marriages with the inhabitants of the land might turn them away from following Him, but it absolutely would (and did). In order for a saved person to have anything in common with an unsaved spouse, they must live the lifestyle of their unsaved spouse. Although many disagree, God's Word always proves itself to be infallible.

For example, consider King Solomon, the wisest man that ever lived under the Old Covenant. Scripture states that Solomon loved God (1 Kings 3:3). He also loved many strange women and took wives from Egypt, Moab, Ammon, Edom, and from the Canaanites. His wives eventually turned his heart after their gods. He went as far as to build high places for the worship of these gods that were still present in Israel many generations later (2 Kings 23:13). None of Solomon's wisdom, or his love for God, kept him when he compromised God's Word. These marriages turned his heart from following God just as God's Word said it would (see 1 Kings 11:1-8). It was also Israel's lack of separation that turned them away from God, and ultimately caused them to be scattered throughout the nations they refused to be separated from.

This has always been a problem for God's people. It remained a problem for Israel even after many of them returned to the land of Israel after the seventy year Babylonian captivity. At first they did separate themselves from what scripture calls the filthiness of the heathen of the land (Ezra 6:19-21); but it was short lived. Ezra 9:1-2 states:

> **Now when these things were done, the princes came to me, saying, The people of Israel, and the priests, and the Levites, have not separated themselves from the people of the lands, <u>doing according to their abominations</u>, even the Canaanites, the Hittites, the Perizzites, the Jebusites, the Ammonites, the Moabites, the Egyptians, and the Amorites. For they have taken of their daughters for themselves, and for their sons: so that the HOLY SEED have mingled themselves with the people of those lands: yea, the hand of the princes and rulers hath been chief in this trespass** (underline and capitals added for emphasis).

This was such a serious matter, under the leadership of Ezra, they made a covenant to put away their strange wives and the children born from them. This was absolutely necessary for them to do, as it was for this reason that God's wrath had previously came upon them to remove them from their land; and His fierce wrath was once again upon them for this transgression. Anyone that would not enter into this covenant forfeited all his substance and was separated from the congregation of Israel (see Ezra chapters 9-10). The book of Nehemiah also records a similar account (Neh. 13).

This is just as much a problem in the church as it was in the nation of Israel. The biblical principle of an unbeliever turning away a believer from following God remains the same. It might not be a complete turning away, but a believer will be greatly affected. Many forfeit much of their spiritual substance, or inheritance, because of this sin. A marriage union under the New Covenant is to be between two that are heirs together of the grace of life (1 Pet. 3:9). A born again believer is to marry ONLY IN THE LORD (1 Cor. 7:39).

Separation from Believers Living in Disobedience

The bible also commands us to separate ourselves from Christian brothers, or those who claim to be Christian brothers, who do not live in obedience to God's Word. Matthew 18:15-17 states:

> **Moreover if thy brother shall trespass against thee, go and tell him his fault between thee and him alone: if he shall hear thee, thou hast gained thy brother. But if he will not hear thee, then take with thee one or two more, that in the mouth of two or three witnesses every word may be established. And if he shall neglect to hear them, tell it unto the church: but if he neglect to hear the church, let him be unto thee as an heathen man and a publican.**

To separate ourselves from a brother in these types of circumstances is for the purpose of convicting him of his sin; and to reveal that his refusal to be reconciled to a brother not only separates him from that brother, but also from God and all those of His family.

Concerning this same subject matter, God's Word states in 2 Thess. 3:6:

> **Now we command you, brethren, in the name of our Lord Jesus Christ, that ye withdraw yourselves from every brother that walketh disorderly, and not after the tradition which he received from us.**

Many members of this church thought that the coming of the Lord was so near that they stopped working, and were living off the other members of the church. The apostle Paul instructs them to work and support themselves (2 Thess. 3:7-13). He then states:

> **And if any man obey not our word by this epistle, note that man, and have no company with him, that he may be ashamed. Yet count him not as an enemy, but admonish him as a brother** (2 Thess. 3:14-15).

1 Corinthians chapter five records an account of a man who was committing fornication with his father's wife (his mother). Many claim that this was most likely his stepmother. In any account, the Apostle Paul called such fornication as an act that was not so much as named among the Gentiles. He instructed them to remove this man from their fellowship stating that a little leaven leavens the whole lump. The Apostle Paul knew that if this man remained in the church, that sin would spread throughout the body.

This is not something to be taken lightly. For example, the sin of homosexuality consumed Sodom and Gomorrah. As proof that God's people are just as much at risk, read Judges Chapters 19-21. The tribe of Benjamin was almost completely destroyed as a result of this sin getting a stronghold in that tribe. Consider also the things that are taking place in the church today. Adultery, fornication, homosexuality, and other sexual immorality are not at all uncommon and are progressively becoming worse. It can only be as a result of not separating ourselves from those who commit such acts. 1 Corinthians 5:9-11 tells us:

> **I wrote unto you in an epistle not to company with fornicators: pany with fornicators: Yet not altogether with the fornicators of this world, or with the covetous, or extortioners, or with idolaters; for then must ye needs go out of the world. But now I have written unto you not to keep company, if any man that is called a brother be a fornicator, or covetous, or an idolater, or a railer, or a drunkard, or an extortioner; with such an one no not to eat.**

Eating is considered one of the highest forms of fellowship in both the Old and New Covenants. When two people share a meal, it is a type of being one with the other. It is also a statement of being in agreement with each other.

Rather than removing those who commit these sins, much of the church today just gives them a slap on the wrist, and encourages them to continue to come to church as a solution to the problem. In so doing, these sins are prevalent and growing in the church.

It is amazing to realize just how many members of the church do not even believe that it would be God's will for us to separate ourselves from such people. After all, how can we help them if we separate ourselves from them? The apostle Paul instructed the Corinthian church to deliver the person committing fornication with his father's wife unto Satan for the destruction of the flesh, that the spirit may be saved in the day of the Lord Jesus (1 Cor. 5:5). Too often we permit people to continue living in sin. Once removed from the church, this man actually repented. It was most likely due to the affliction that he suffered as a result of being delivered unto Satan for the destruction of his flesh.

In his second letter to this church, Paul instructs them to forgive this man, comfort him, and receive him back into their fellowship (2 Cor. 2:6-8). The act of separating themselves from this man not only kept the church secure, but also brought this man to repentance.

Romans 16:17 tells us to mark them which cause divisions and offences contrary to the doctrine that we have received, and avoid them. The Word also states that if anyone comes unto us and does not bring the doctrine of Christ, we are not to receive him into our house, or bid him God speed (2 Jn. 10).

God's Word also warns us that in the last days perilous times shall come (to the church, 2 Tim. 3:1).

> **For men shall be lovers of their own selves, covetous, boasters, proud, blasphemers, disobedient to parents, unthankful, unholy, Without natural affection, trucebreakers, false accusers, incontinent, fierce, despisers of those that are good, Traitors, heady, high-minded, lovers of pleasure more than lovers of God; Having a form of godliness, but denying the power thereof: from such turn away** (2 Tim. 3: 2-5).

As these have a form of godliness, this is not speaking of the condition of the world, but of the church. We are commanded to turn away from all such (so called) believers.

As we can clearly see, God has commanded us to be a separated people for some very important reasons. It helps us keep sin out of our lives, it keeps us from being corrupted by the world, and keeps us from turning away from God. It also brings conviction in the lives of others that actually draws them to God.

Chapter 12

THE PEOPLE'S CHOICE

It is a very normal thing to want to be in control of our own lives and destiny; but just how much are we really capable when it comes to living a Christian life? Jeremiah 10:23 states, **"O LORD, I know that the way of man is not in himself: it is not in man that walketh to direct his steps."** Few of us realize the importance of God intervening into our lives. To begin with, if He would never intervene into our lives, no one would ever come unto salvation. Many people might disagree with that statement, but it is made very clear in God's Word. Jesus stated, **"No man can come unto me, except the Father which hath sent me draw him: and I will raise him up at the last day"** (Jn. 6:44).

This is clearly seen with the nation of Israel whom God chose to be His people. He actually made Himself their God. Concerning all the other nations, Acts 14:16 states, **"Who in times past suffered all nations to walk in their own ways."** No other nation turned to the one true God of Israel by letting them walk in their own way. It was not in their nature to do so. If God would have left it up to Israel they would have also went the way of all the other nations. They even tried to return to Egypt (a type of the world) shortly after they were delivered from it, but God would not permit them to do so (Num. 14:4). They continually turned away from God and worshipped the gods of the other nations. They were the only nation to change their God (Jer. 2:11). There was always a desire to return to (or be like) the world.

To Be Like All The Nations

At first God set up Judges in the nation of Israel to judge His people, but He was to reign as their King. The last of these Judges was the prophet Samuel. When Samuel grew old he made his sons Judges over Israel, but they did not walk in his ways. They went after lucre (money), took bribes, and perverted judgment (1 Sam. 8:1-3). This gave the elders in Israel the opportunity they desired, which was to be like all the other nations. They came to Samuel and said unto him, **"Behold, thou art old, and thy sons walk not in thy ways: now make us a king to judge us like all the nations"** (1 Sam. 8:5).

This displeased Samuel, but the Lord said unto him:

> **Hearken unto the voice of the people in all that they say unto thee: for they have not rejected thee, but they have rejected me, that I should not reign over them. According to all the works which they have done since the day that I brought them up out of Egypt even unto this day, wherewith they have forsaken me, and served other gods, so do they also unto thee. Now therefore hearken unto their voice: howbeit yet protest solemnly unto them, and shew them the manner of the king that shall reign over them** (1 Sam. 8:7-9).

Samuel then told the people the consequences of having a king, and what they would lose as a result. Their king would take their sons to reap his harvest, and to be his instruments of war. He would take their daughters for confectionaries, cooks, and bakers. He would take the best of their fields, vineyards, and olive yards for his servants. He would take the tenth (which is God's, Lev. 27: 30) of their seed, vineyards, and sheep to give to his officers and servants. The people of Israel would be his servants (1 Sam. 8:18).

> **Nevertheless the people refused to obey the voice of Samuel; and they said, Nay, but we will have a king over us; THAT WE ALSO MAY BE LIKE ALL THE NATIONS; and that our king may judge us, and go out before us, and fight our battles** (1 Sam. 8:19-20). (Capitals added for emphasis).

They wanted a king to take God's place. God therefore gave them a king. He gave them a man named Saul from the tribe of Benjamin. Concerning Saul, 1 Samuel 9:2 states:

> **And he had a son, whose name was Saul, a choice young man, and a goodly: and there was not among the children of Israel a goodlier person than he: from his shoulders and upward he was higher than any of the people.**

When God revealed to Samuel who their king was to be, Samuel took a vial of oil, poured it upon Saul's head, and anointed him to be captain (king) over Israel (1 Sam. 10:1).

When Samuel presented Saul to Israel, he said, "**Now therefore behold the king WHOM YE HAVE CHOSEN, and whom ye have desired! and, behold, the LORD hath set a king over you**" (1 Sam. 12:13). (Capitals added for emphasis.) Saul was the people's choice. They asked for a king, and God gave them the king of their choice and desire. The name Saul actually means: asked, prayed for, and desired.

Soon after beginning his reign, Saul offered a burnt offering and a peace offering, which only the priest could offer. He did this in his lack of patience in waiting for Samuel (who was a priest), and his fear that God would not be with him in an upcoming battle against the Philistines (1 Sam. 13:1-12).

This fear could only be a result of a sinful lifestyle before God. When Samuel then arrived, he told Saul:

> **Thou hast done foolishly: thou hast not kept the commandment of the LORD thy God, which he commanded thee: for now would the LORD have established thy kingdom upon Israel forever. But now thy kingdom shall not continue: the LORD hath sought him a man after his own heart, and the LORD hath commanded him to be captain over his people, because thou hast not kept that which the LORD commanded thee** (1 Sam. 13:13-14).

Saul again disobeyed God's Word in a battle with the Amalekites. God commanded him to destroy everything, but Saul spared the king of Amalek, and the best of the livestock to offer sacrifices unto God. This time God rejected him as being king. 1 Sam. 15:22-24 states:

> **And Samuel said, Hath the LORD as great delight in burnt-offering and sacrifices, as in obeying the voice of the LORD? Behold, to obey is better than sacrifice, and to hearken than the fat of rams. For rebellion is as the sin of witchcraft, and stubbornness is as iniquity and idolatry. Because thou hast rejected the word of the LORD, he hath also rejected thee from being king. And Saul said unto Samuel, I have sinned: for I have transgressed the commandment of the LORD, and thy words: because I feared the people, and obeyed their voice.**

The people chose a king according to his outward appearance, one that did not keep God's Word, and one that obeyed their voice.

God's Choice

God then instructed Samuel to take a horn of oil, and anoint a son of a man named Jesse to be king over Israel. Jesse had eight sons. As Samuel looked upon the eldest, he said:

> **Surely the LORD'S anointed is before him. But the LORD said unto Samuel, Look not on his countenance, or on the height of his stature; because I have refused him: for the LORD seeth not as man seeth; for man looketh on the outward appearance, but the LORD looketh on the heart** (1 Sam. 16:6-7).

God's choice of a king was not to be like Saul, whose out-ward appearance and height was better and greater than any other among the children of Israel. His choice was a shepherd boy named David, the youngest and least likely to be chosen from a worldly or human perspective. The name David means "beloved". He was the man after God's own heart because he loved the Lord, and lived in obedience to His Word.

It is also important to understand the difference of how these two men were anointed to be king, both by Samuel. God told Samuel to anoint Saul with a vial of oil, but David with a horn of oil. A vial is a symbol of God's wrath (Revelation chapters 15-16). Hundreds of years later, in reference to Saul, Hosea 13:10-11 states:

> **I will be thy king: where is any other that may save thee in all thy cities? and thy judges of whom thou saidst, Give me a king and princes? I gave thee a king in my anger, and took him away in my wrath.**

On the other hand, a horn is a symbol of power and strength. The nation of Israel was originally designed to be a theocracy. A theocracy is a government ruled by God. Saul began the period of the monarchy, where the rule of God was to be carried on through the role of a king. However, many ungodly kings caused the people to fall away and forsake God. The people desired a democracy, which is a government by the people, exercised through elected officials. It is where the majority rules with the common people being considered the primary source of political power. As God's people are only a remnant compared to those of any nation, a democracy is not of God, and will always lead to an ungodly nation. Look at what has taken place in America. There is separation between church and state. Many consider the words 'under God' in the pledge of allegiance unconstitutional. Prayer has been removed from schools and the Ten Commandments from courthouses. The list goes on and on. We have become a nation that does not like to retain God in our knowledge (Rom. 1:28), and clearly do not want God to reign over us.

Without God, We Would All Do The Same

Do not think that it is any different with us today. If God just let us walk after our own ways, we would all continue to walk according to the course of this world, according to the prince of the power of the air (Satan), the spirit that now works in the children of disobedience. We would continue to walk in the lusts of our flesh, fulfilling the desires of the flesh and of the mind (Eph. 2:2-3). God works in the lives of His chosen people to bring them unto salvation, and then keeps them afterward by His power unto the completion of that salvation (1 Pet. 1:5).

We are no different from those of Israel who chose Barabbas instead of Christ. There is more to this than most of us realize. The name Barabbas means: son of the father. At one point, Jesus stated, **"I am come in my Father's name, and ye receive me not: if another shall come in his own name, him ye will receive."** Jesus, who was the Son of the Father, was rejected. Barabbas, who came in his own name, (which means son of the father) was received. It is also interesting to see what the different gospels say of him. The gospel of John calls him a robber. The book of Mark and Luke wrote that he was in prison for insurrection (sedition) and murder. He is therefore a type of the devil who comes to steal, kill and destroy (Jn. 10:10). If left to walk in our own ways, we would all chose the prince of the power of the air, the spirit that works in all unsaved men.

The church is also no different from Israel in wanting to be like the world. Many do not want God to reign over their lives. They consider it their life. They want to be Christians but still live their lives like the people of the world. Those who do so reject God from being their King. They become just like those of Israel who did that which was right in their own eyes (Jud. 17:6, 21: 25). God's Word tells us, "**There is a way that seemeth right unto a man, but the end thereof are the ways of death**" (Pro. 16:25).

When Israel was to cross over the Jordan into their inheritance, which is a type of our salvation, Moses told them, "**Ye shall not do after all the things that we do here today, every man whatsoever is right in his own eyes**" (Deut. 12:8). After salvation we are to change the way we previously lived our lives. We need to make sure that the choices we make are in obedience and in harmony with God's Word. This is where God's thoughts and will are revealed to us. We have a tendency to think that God is like us, but according to scripture, He is not (Ps. 50:21). Isaiah 55:8-9 states:

> **For my thoughts are not your thoughts, neither are your ways my ways, saith the LORD, For as the heavens are higher than the earth, so are my ways higher than your ways, and my thoughts than your thoughts.**

Any choices we make according to the course of this world, or the lusts of the flesh, will lead us away from God. We should endeavor to have God reign over every detail of our lives.

Chapter 13

REPAIRING THE BREACHES IN OUR LIVES

A breach is a gap, break, leak, rip, opening or fracture. The bible usually speaks of a breach as a gap, break or opening in a wall that the enemy uses to enter a city or building. God's Word often speaks of walled cities, and their importance, as places of refuge against an attack from an enemy. The walled city of Jericho was the first stronghold that Israel faced when they entered into the land of their inheritance. It could have taken months, maybe even years, to conquer Jericho without God's intervention. The walls of Jericho had to come down to give Israel quick access into the city (Joshua. 6). In most instances, a fenced city had to come under siege by an army that would let nothing come in or go out until the inhabitants were forced to surrender or starve. The only other way to conquer a walled city was to find a weak place and make a breach in the wall.

This has real significance in our lives as Christians. There are important lessons taught concerning this in the books of Ezra and Nehemiah. The book of Ezra teaches us about the rebuilding of God's temple in Jerusalem after many of the Israelite captives returned after the seventy year Babylonian captivity. The temple was rebuilt under heavy persecution from those of the other nations that then inhabited the land.

The persecution began from the time that the foundation of the temple was laid (Ezra chapters 3-6).

The temples built under the Old Covenant were a type of the church. The New Testament often refers to the church as a temple, or building, with Jesus Christ as the chief corner stone, and born again believers as the stones that build up the temple (Eph. 2:19-22, Heb. 3:1-6, 1 Pet. 2:4-7). The bodies of individual believers are also referred to as temples of God or of the Holy Spirit (1 Cor. 3:16-17, 6:19-20, 2 Cor. 6:16). Jesus Christ is also referred to as the foundation that has been laid, and which is to be built upon (1 Cor. 3:11).

The book of Nehemiah teaches us about the rebuilding of the walls of Jerusalem after the temple was rebuilt. The rebuilding of the walls was also done under heavy persecution from Israel's enemies. They were under constant threat of war the entire time. Each one worked with his sword girded by his side.

Building and Repairing the Breaches in Our Temple

The valuable lessons taught in these books teach us what we need to do in our own lives. Upon receiving Jesus Christ at salvation, our bodies become temples of God. Each of us becomes workers and laborers together with God to build His house, and repair the breaches that are within. 1 Cor. 3:9-11 states:

> **For we are labourers together with God: ye are God's husbandry, ye are God's building. According to the grace of God which is given unto me, as a wise master builder, I have laid the foundation, and another buildeth thereon. But let every man take heed how he buildeth thereupon. For other foundation can no man lay than that is laid, which is Jesus Christ.**
> (See also 2 Corinthians 6:1.)

Just as seen in the building of the temple as recorded in the book of Ezra, the persecution and attacks from the enemy begin as soon as the foundation of our salvation is laid. As gone over earlier, this foundation is Jesus Christ. We enter into a spiritual warfare where our enemy constantly searches our lives to find a weakness where he can gain access. For example, he will often find access into our lives by the words we speak. Proverbs 15:4 states, **"A wholesome tongue is a tree of life: but perverseness therein is a breach in the spirit."**

We are to constantly build ourselves up against the attacks from the enemy. The best way to do this is by learning God's Word (our sword) and walking in obedience to it. The rejection of God's Word in any area of one's life is iniquity that can cause a breach that can break off and fall at any time. Isa. 30:12-13 says:

> **Wherefore thus saith the Holy One of Israel, Because ye despise this word, and trust in oppression and perverseness, and stay thereon: Therefore this iniquity shall be to you as a breach ready to fall, swelling out in a high wall, whose breaking cometh suddenly at an instant.**

Even after a temple was built, over a period of time, there would appear breaches in the wall. We have such an example recorded in God's Word during the reign of King Josiah. He commanded the high priest to take the silver (which is a type of God's redeemed, Ex. 30:12-13, 38:25-28), which was brought into the house of the Lord, and delivered it to the carpenters, builders, and masons to repair the breaches in the temple (2 Ki. 22: 3-7). The breach is a type of sin in the life of a believer. God's builders and laborers of the New Covenant are to repair the breaches through the preaching and teaching God's Word. They are also to live a holy life as an example for others to follow. No believer is excluded from this as we have all been foreordained by God to do good works (Eph. 2:10).

Building and Closing the Breaches in Our Walls

As found in the book of Nehemiah, we also need to build walls and set up gates that will fortify our temples. This is a labor, and as those who built the wall around Jerusalem, a person must have a mind to work (Neh. 4:7). This work will also come under attack from our adversaries as each thing we do to bring our lives in obedience to God's Word closes a breach in our wall (Neh. 4:7).

Just as the wall was to protect Jerusalem from the people of the other nations, we build our spiritual wall by separating ourselves from the world and those who live ungodly lifestyles. We set up our gates when we only let into our lives that which pertain to a holy life. Everything else needs to be shut out.

The bible says that the strength of those who built the wall was diminished as a result of all the rubbish from when the wall was earlier destroyed by the army of Babylon. These piles of rubbish were used by the enemy to set up an attack against God's people to cause the work to cease (Neh. 4:10-11). There is also much rubbish that needs to be cleaned up in our own lives as we fortify the wall around our temple. We clean up our rubbish as we forsake our old lifestyle and fleshly lusts.

Someone to Stand in the Breach

As the wall was previously torn down as a result of the sin of Israel, sin in our own life will cause us to be conquered by our adversaries and our wall to be torn down. It is obvious that every believer is not going to strive to keep sin out of his or her lives. This makes it very important that some of us do.

For example, when Israel came out of Egypt they made and worshipped golden calf. God would have destroyed them had not Moses stood before Him in the breach to turn away His wrath (Ps. 106:19-23). Before His wrath came against Israel for their sins, Ezek. 22:30 states, **"And I** sought for a man among them, that should make up the hedge, and stand in the gap before me for the land, that I should not destroy it: but I found none."

Of course, Jesus is the man that now stands in that gap, but it is also our responsibility to be there with Him. God's Word says that we are to be called, **"The repairer of the breach, The restorer of paths to dwell in"** (Isa. 58:12).

Chapter 14

BE CAREFUL WHAT YOU EAT

The first provision that God made for man was the food he was to eat, both naturally and spiritually. Eating is a very important subject matter spoken of throughout God's Word. It is often a spiritual act. It was through the act of eating that sin entered into the world. God's Word teaches us about two different kinds of food. There is the food that sustains the natural body, and the spiritual food that feeds the soul and causes us to grow spiritually. A person must eat to sustain his spiritual life as well as his natural.

Eating Produced the Spiritual State of Man

The bible says that God formed man of the dust of the ground; breathed into his nostrils the breath of life, and man became a living soul (Gen. 2:7). The following verse speaks of God planting a garden in Eden where He put the man whom He had formed. Gen. 2:9 then states:

> **And out of the ground made the LORD God to grow every tree that is pleasant to the sight, and good for food; the tree of life also in the midst of the garden, and the tree of knowledge of good and evil.**

The trees that God made to grow out of the ground produced the food, which was to sustain the natural body. The Word then speaks of two other trees that were also in the garden: the tree of life, and the tree of knowledge of good and evil. The spiritual state of man was to be determined by which of these two trees the man would eat of.

After placing the man in the garden God commanded him, saying:

Of every tree of the garden thou mayest freely eat: But of the tree of the knowledge of good and evil, thou shalt not eat of it: for in the day that thou eatest thereof thou shalt surely die (Gen. 2:16-17).

We know from Genesis chapter three that the serpent tempted Eve, and as a result man ate from the tree of the knowledge of good and evil (Gen. 3:1-6). Man died spiritually at the very moment he ate of the forbidden tree, and entered into the kingdom of darkness, Satan's domain.

All Are Fruit Bearing Trees

A diligent study of God's Word reveals that the tree of life is in reference to Christ, as He is the only source of life for man (Jn. 1:4, 6:48-58, 1 Jn. 1:1-2). Therefore the tree of the knowledge of good and evil must be in reference to Satan. This is also revealed in God's Word, which speaks of man as having received the same spirit and nature of Satan as a result of eating of the tree of the knowledge of good and evil (Eph. 2:2-3). Unsaved men are also spoken of as being the children of the devil (Jn. 8:44, 1 Jn. 3:9-10). The book of 1 John makes it quite clear that there are only two kinds of people in the world: the children of God, and the children of the devil (1 Jn. 3:8-10).

It is therefore not at all unusual for the bible to refer to men as trees. After all, we all bear fruit. What type of fruit we bear depends upon what kind of tree we are. Jesus stated:

> Even so every good tree bringeth forth good fruit; but a corrupt tree bringeth forth evil fruit. A good tree cannot bring forth evil fruit, neither can a corrupt tree bring forth good fruit. Every tree that bringeth not forth good fruit is hewn down, and cast into the fire. Wherefore by their fruits ye shall know them (Matt. 7:17-20).

The good trees are the children of God. The corrupt trees are the children of the devil. We will find that it is only God's children that can bring forth good fruit. Good fruit can only be brought forth through God's Spirit (Gal. 5:22). All other fruit is evil as it is produced from the sinful spirits (nature) of unsaved men.

So, what was the fruit of the knowledge of good and evil? Could it have been the lies the serpent used to tempt and beguile Eve? Speaking of the sin of Israel, Hosea 10:13 states:

> Ye have plowed wickedness, ye have reaped iniquity; YE HAVE EATEN THE FRUIT OF LIES: because thou didst trust in thy way, in the multitude of thy mighty men.

Scripture often refers to spoken words as being fruit.

Proverbs 18:20-21 states:

> A man's belly shall be satisfied with the fruit of his mouth; and with the increase of his lips shall he be filled. Death and life are in the power of the tongue: and they that love it shall eat the fruit thereof.

We will find that words are the spiritual man's food. Pro. 10:21 states:

> The lips of the righteous feed many: but fools die for want of wisdom. Pro. 13: 2-3 also states, **A man shall**

eat good by the fruit of his mouth: but the soul of the transgressors shall eat violence. He that keepeth his mouth keepeth his life: but he that openeth wide his lips shall have destruction.

Violence, anger, wrath, hatred, and such like are all the results of the words that a person is eating or has eaten of.

Words Are The Spiritual Man's Food

Words are what feed the spirit because they are spirit. Jesus stated, "**It is the spirit that quickeneth; the flesh profiteth nothing: the words that I speak unto you, they are spirit, and they are life**" (Jn. 6:63). Just as the words of God are spirit and life, the words of the enemy are spirit and death. That is why man died in the day he ate of the tree of the knowledge of good and evil, and became by nature children of God's wrath (Eph. 2:1-3). Words are the same spirit as the one who speaks them. To eat of God's Word is to partake of His Spirit. To eat of Satan's words is to partake of His spirit.

It still remains that man must eat of the tree of life to receive God's Spirit. That is why Jesus Christ is so vitally important in God's plan of salvation. Let's consider the Passover Lamb that pointed to Jesus Christ, the true Lamb of God (Jn. 1:29). The Passover lamb not only had to be killed, and the blood put on the two side posts and on the upper door post of each house, but the flesh of the lamb had to be eaten that same night.

With this in mind, let's look at what Jesus taught in John chapter six, which took place when the Feast of Passover was near (Jn. 6:4). The bulk of this entire chapter deals with eating. Those of Israel wanted a sign from Him, and made reference to the manna that their fathers ate in the wilderness. They referred to it as the bread that came down from heaven. The manna itself was a type of God's Word (Deut. 8:3). Jesus then stated that He was the true bread of God that came down from heaven to give life to the world. He went on to say that He was the bread of life that a man may eat thereof, and not die. He declared His flesh to be that bread. Whoever would eat of His flesh and drink of His blood would have eternal life, as they would then dwell in Him, and He would dwell in them (Jn. 6:30-58).

What exactly did Jesus mean by stating that a person must eat of His flesh and drink of His blood to have eternal life? The answer is found in the first chapter of the gospel of John. Jn. 1:1 states:

> **In the beginning was the Word, and the Word was with God, and the Word was God.** Jn. 1:14 then states, **And the Word was made flesh, and dwelt among us, (and we beheld his glory, the glory as of the only begotten Son of the Father,) full of grace and truth.**

Jesus Christ is the Word of God (that was made flesh). We can never separate the Word of God from Jesus Christ for they are one and the same. We must eat of the gospel message of Jesus Christ to receive salvation (Romans 1:16, 10:8-10). 1 Pet. 1:23 states, **"Being born again, not of corruptible seed, but of incorruptible, by the word of God, which liveth and abideth forever."** Jesus did not mean that we were to eat of His literal flesh, and drink of His literal blood, but to eat of His Word and drink of His Spirit. As His words are Spirit, we drink of His Spirit as we eat of His Word (1 Cor. 12:13). Just as the life of the natural flesh (body) is in the blood (Lev. 17:11), the life of the body of Christ is in His Spirit.

You Are What You Eat

After salvation we must continue to eat of God's Word consistently to grow to maturity. The saying, 'You are what you eat' is very true. Our natural bodies consist of the food we have eaten. The food we ate as children produce the substance that was needed for our bodies to grow. Our bodies are now maintained from the substance of the food we eat.

It works the same way spiritually. As newborn babes we are to desire the sincere milk of the Word that we may grow thereby (1 Peter 2:2). As we mature spiritually, we need to continue to eat of the meat of the Word to maintain our growth and strength (Heb. 5:12-14). To be conformed into the image of Jesus Christ is to become the Word (Christ), which we have eaten. God's Word states, "**Man shall not live by bread alone, but by every word that proceedeth out of the mouth of God**" (Matt. 4:4). We will either feed the Spirit of God within us, or the spirit of the enemy which works through the sinful nature of the flesh. Whichever one is fed the most will be the most dominant. Believers who feed their flesh more than their born again Spirit will walk according to the flesh, and live carnal lives.

Believers need to be very careful of the words we eat of. Most believers take this far too lightly, especially in the world we live in today. So many are under the false impression that what they read, listen to, talk about, or watch on TV does not really affect them spiritually. Nothing could be farther from the truth. A lot of what we read that does not pertain to God's Word feeds the sinful nature of the flesh. As God's Word gradually renews our minds, reading worldly books and magazines will keep us carnally minded and gradually works more ungodliness into our lives. A little leaven does leaven the whole lump (1 Cor. 5: 6). For those who just enjoy reading, the bible is an inexhaustible source of wisdom, knowledge, and understanding. One can also enjoy reading the bible as much as any novel. It is filled with true stories of suspense, drama, action, and love. It should never grow old as one can receive more insight each time it is read.

We Eat of the Music We Listen To

Music is also very spiritual. For example, when King Nebuchadnezzar (of Babylon) made an image of gold, he commanded it to be worshipped when the sound of the musical instruments was heard (Dan. 3:1-5). A person will enjoy and listen to the kind of music that best agrees with him spiritually. Believers who desire and listen to any kind of worldly music instead of music that pertains to the praise and worship of God will be carnal Christians. Many types of music are clearly demonic. Others are far less conspicuous, but still promote the ungodly spirit of the world. Even so called Christian rock and rap music are taken from the world, and are designed by the enemy to hold us in bondage to the world and the flesh.

Eating as we Watch Television

Television can be detrimental in the life of a believer, and keeps many believers walking in carnality. Just look at how it has even changed the world we live in today. For example, not too long ago, any kind of witchcraft was considered unacceptable in our society. Then there began to appear television shows like 'Bewitched' that began to change the way witchcraft was previously thought of. Even the Wonderful World of Disney began to make movies filled with witchcraft. All these portrayed witchcraft as good, fun, and useful. Witchcraft such as Wicca is now an accepted religion in the United States today, and is considered completely constitutional under the Freedom of Religion clause.

This has not only affected the world but has also infiltrated into the church. The things many Christians watch on TV is astonishing. Although many good churches do speak out against movies like the Harry Potter series, many others see them as harmless entertainment. According to God's Word, we should tolerate no witchcraft of any kind. To do so is to feed us with that spirit.

Almost all of the evening comedy shows, and most movies, portray casual sex as an acceptable lifestyle. That is now the way that it is thought of in much of the world. Even many Christians don't seem to think that sex outside of marriage is that big of a deal. We have accepted more of what we see on TV than what the Word of God teaches. As a result, sexual sin is rampant in the church today. When we sit in front of the TV set we are feeding ourselves with whatever we are watching.

Just as faith comes by hearing, and hearing by the Word of God (Rom. 10: 17), doubt also comes by hearing the word of the enemy. Whatever we feed our flesh with fights against God's Word effectually working in our lives. **"For the flesh lusteth against the Spirit, and the Spirit against the flesh: and these are contrary the one to the other: so that ye cannot do the things that ye would"** (Gal. 5:17). There are certain things that Christians just shouldn't do.

We Eat as We Converse with Each Other

We can also feed ourselves with the ungodly conversations that are so easy to get caught up in. God's Word instructs us to be a separated people for some very good reasons. Those who do not live separated lives from the people of the world do get drawn away from following God (Ex. 23:33, Deut. 7:1-4). Those who are not born again cannot receive or know the things that pertain to God's Spirit (1 Cor. 2:1-4). They have no ability to speak the words that we need spiritually. They can only talk of worldly things, and will most generally tear us down spiritually. God's Word even instructs us to separate ourselves from those who claim they are Christians, but are clearly living in sin (1 Cor. 5:9-11).

Eating is a Spiritual Act

To eat with someone is a spiritual act of fellowship. When two people share a meal together, they are saying that they are in agreement with each other. As they eat together, and the food enters their bodies, it is an action saying I am one with this person. This is why it is important to share meals with family members and those in the body of Christ, but not with all. It was a common practice under the Old Covenant. Those of Israel did not eat with those of other nations (Acts 10:28, 11:3).

Israel's priests were also instructed to eat a portion of many of the sacrifices offered unto God in the holy place, the court of the tabernacle. Remember, we are all priests unto God under the New Covenant (1 Pet.

2:5, Rev. 1:6). A portion of the offering was offered unto God by being burnt on the altar. This was called the food of the offering by fire unto the Lord (Lev. 3:11). The priests' portion was then to be eaten in the holy place as a type of them eating with God. As each offering pointed to the work of Christ, each time we study God's Word we are eating from His table.

Chapter 15

BE CAREFUL WHAT YOU SPEAK

The bible says that death and life are in the power of the tongue (Prov. 18:20). As believers, we need to be very careful of the words we speak for many reasons. There is power in spoken words. It does not matter if they are meant for good or evil. The words we speak will greatly affect and determine the course of our lives. The power of the words that God speaks will help us to better understand this. God's Word has created everything in existence. Whatever God says is sure. His Word never returns to Him void, and always accomplishes that which He sends it to do (Isa. 55:11).

Born again believers have God's Spirit. We are to be led by God's Spirit in everything we do and say. The words we speak by God's Spirit will also not return void, and accomplish that which they are sent to do. However, everything we speak has an impact in our lives and in the lives of others. We will either speak words that originate from faith or unbelief. Our words will either build up or tear down. All will affect our lives.

The Words We Speak Come Out Of The Heart

> O generation of vipers, how can ye, being evil, speak good things? for out of the abundance of the heart the mouth speaketh. A good man out of the good treasure of the heart bringeth forth good things: and an evil man out of the evil treasure bringeth forth evil things. But I say unto you, That every idle word that men shall speak, they shall give account thereof in the day of judgment. For by thy words thou shalt be justified, and by thy words thou shalt be condemned (Matt. 12:34-37).

In the Day of Judgment each one of us must give an account of every idle word that we have spoken. The word translated here as idle means to be inactive, useless or barren. That means that every word we speak should be active, useful and bear fruit. It will be by the words we speak that we will later be justified (declared innocent) or condemned.

We also see from this passage of scripture that what is in a person's heart is what they will speak out of their mouth. This must be why God's Word instructs us to keep our hearts will all diligence; for out of it are the issues of life (Pro. 4:23). It must also be one of the reasons why scripture speaks of the importance of us having God's Word in our hearts. Deut. 6:6-7 states:

> And these words, which I command thee this day, shall be in thine heart. And thou shalt teach them diligently unto thy children, and shalt talk of them when thou sittest in thine house, and when thou walkest by the way, and when thou liest down, and when thou risest up.

Once God's Word is in a person's heart, that is what he will speak out of his mouth. As we can see, there should never be a time, activity, or place where we should not be speaking of God's Word. It should always be our main topic of conversation. Ps. 119:11 also states, **"Thy word have I hid in mine heart, that I might not sin against thee."**

Christians should have the most wholesome language of any other people. Eph. 4:29-31 states:

> **Let no corrupt communication proceed out of your mouth, but that which is good to the use of edifying, that it may minister grace to the hearers. And grieve not the Holy Spirit of God, whereby ye are sealed unto the day of redemption. Let all bitterness, and wrath, and anger, and clamour, and evil speaking, be put away from you, with all malice.**

There is never an excuse for a child of God to speak evil or with profanity. Any bitterness, wrath, or anger that is in a person's heart will eventually be spoken out of their mouth. The words that a person speaks not only reveal what's truly in their heart, but also show the condition of their spirit. We are to cleanse ourselves from all filthiness of the flesh and spirit (2 Cor. 7:1).

The Results of Murmuring and Complaining

Christians should be the most edifying, positive people on the earth. Murmuring is one of the worst things a Christian can do. Phil. 2:14-15 states:

> **Do all things without murmurings and disputings: that ye may be blameless and harmless, the sons of God, without rebuke, in the midst of a crooked and perverse nation, among whom ye shine as lights in the world.**

We can see some of the tragic effects of murmuring by what took place with the nation of Israel soon after they were delivered from Egypt. As soon as three days after crossing the Red Sea they began to murmur because they had found no water to drink. They came to a place called Marah, for the water there was bitter and they could not drink it. Ex. 15:24-25 then states:

> **And the people murmured against Moses, saying, What shall we drink? And he cried unto the LORD; and the LORD shewed him a tree, which when he had cast into the waters, the waters were made sweet: there he made for them a statute and an ordinance, and there he proved them.**

The bitter waters show that we will suffer bitter experiences as a result of our Christian walk. There are the trials, afflictions, temptations and persecutions that we must all endure. The tree that made the waters sweet represents the cross of Christ that takes the bitterness out of all such experiences. It reminds us that all we go through is God's will for our lives. This removes any reason for us to complain or murmur.

It was not long before they murmured about their lack of food. Ex. 16:2-3 states:

> **And the whole congregation of the children of Israel murmured against Moses and Aaron in the wilderness: And the children of Israel said unto them, Would to God we had died by the hand of the LORD in the land of Egypt, when we sat by the flesh pots, and when we did eat bread to the full; for ye have brought us forth into this wilderness, to kill this whole assembly with hunger.**

This is when God promised to rain bread from heaven for them to eat, which later became known as the manna. The manna is a type of God's Word that he has given to feed us spiritually under the New Covenant

(Deut. 8:3, Matt. 4:4). This also makes it a type of Christ, the Word made flesh (Jn. 1:14, 6:31-35).

Moses then informed the congregation of Israel that God was hearing their murmurings against Him. Even though their murmurings were directed toward Moses and Aaron, they were actually murmuring against the Lord. Ex. 16:8b states, **"for that the LORD heareth your murmurings which ye murmur against him: and what are we? your murmurings are not against us, but against the LORD."** When we murmur as Christians, it is against God who promises to take care of us and supply all our needs. He remains in sovereign control over our lives. To murmur is to insinuate that you are not satisfied with God's provision for you, or what He is doing in your life. We are to pray and give thanks for all things, not murmur.

The children of Israel once again murmured for water in their lack of trust for God to continue to supply their needs. They gave little thought or consideration to what God had done for them up to this point. Ex. 17:2-3 states:

> **Wherefore the people did chide with Moses, and said, Give us water that we may drink. And Moses said unto them, Why chide ye with me? wherefore do ye tempt the LORD? And the people thirsted there for water; and the people murmured against Moses, and said, Wherefore is this that thou hast brought us up out of Egypt, to kill us and our children and our cattle with thirst?**

As God had already proved them at the waters of Marah, to murmur now was to tempt Him. This is when God told Moses to smite the rock in Horeb, and water came out for the people to drink.

> **And he called the name of the place Massah, and Meribah, because of the chiding of the children of**

> Israel, and because they tempted the LORD, saying, Is the LORD among us, or not? (Ex. 17:7).

We learn from the New Testament that the Rock, which Moses struck was Christ (1 Cor. 10:4). Smiting the Rock represented the crucifixion. As a result, the water of the Holy Spirit flows from Christ to completely satisfy our spiritual thirst for God. It is also proof that God is among us. The Israelites continued to complain and murmur throughout their entire journey as God led them to their promised land. This displeased God and caused His anger and wrath to be kindled against them (Num. 11:1). When they got tired of the manna they complained about that, and wanted to eat meat as they had in Egypt. God gave them quails to eat, which many lusted after bringing God's wrath against them. Many died as a result of the plague (Numbers chapter 11).

Once they arrived at the border of their promised land they sent out twelve spies to spy out the land. Ten of them brought back an evil report, saying:

> We be not able to go up against the people; for they are stronger than we. And they brought up an evil report of the land which they had searched unto the children of Israel, saying, The land, through which we have gone to search it, is a land that eateth up the inhabitants thereof; and the people that we saw in it are men of great stature. And there we saw the giants, the sons of Anak, which came of the giants: and we were in our own sight as grasshoppers, and so we were in their sight.

This caused the whole congregation of the children of Israel to murmur against Moses and Aaron, saying:

> Would God we had died in the land of Egypt! or would God we had died in the wilderness! And wherefore

> hath the LORD brought us into this land, to fall by the sword, that our wives and our children should be a prey? were it not better for us to return into Egypt? (Num. 14:2b-3).

They then decided to make them a captain and return to Egypt. Of course God intervened and did not permit that to take place.

We Receive What We Speak in God's Ears

As a result of this rebellion, the first generation that came out of Egypt was not permitted to enter into their promised land. Num. 14:26-29 states:

> And the LORD spake unto Moses and unto Aaron, saying, How long shall I bear with this evil congregation, which murmur against me? I have heard the murmurings of the children of Israel, which they murmur against me. Say unto them, As truly as I live, saith the LORD, AS YE HAVE SPOKEN IN MINE EARS, SO WILL I DO TO YOU: Your car cases shall fall in this wilderness; and all that were numbered of you, according to your whole number, from twenty years old and upward, which have murmured against me. (Capital letters added for emphasis.)

They continued to speak the words declaring that God had brought them out of Egypt to kill them with thirst, hunger, or the sword in the wilderness. God therefore gave them what they spoke in His ears. All that generation died in the wilderness over the next forty years. When Moses was later preparing the second generation to go into the land, he reminded them how the words of the ten spies had discouraged the heart of the children of Israel from going over into the land which the Lord had given them (Num. 32:7-9).

We often read about these things in the Old Testament, and wonder how the nation of Israel, after all that God had done for them, acted in the way they did. It's not much different in the church today. In spite of all God's blessings, we also murmur and complain about everything that displeases us. It seems like ten out of twelve church members speak words that discourage the heart of other members rather than encourage, edify, or build them up in faith. How often do we go to a brother or sister looking for a second witness or some encouragement, but walk away with doubt and disappointment planted in our heart instead?

The church is filled with those who murmur and complain about everything that does not go according to their plans. We must come to the understanding that our murmurings are against God, who will eventually give us what we speak in His ear.

Chapter 16

KNOWING GOD'S WILL

Many speak of God's will as if it is some mysterious thing that we can never truly know or understand. A study of God's Word will reveal that this is really not the case. Although there is a secret will of God, the revealed will of God is clearly taught in scripture. Deut. 29:29 states, **"The secret things belong unto the LORD our God: but those things which are revealed belong unto us and to our children for ever, that we may do all the words of this law."** Every believer is held accountable to live his or her life according to the revealed will of God. There is nothing hidden or mysterious about it. It is clearly laid out for us in God's Word.

Knowing God's Will Through His Word

God actually expects us to come to know and understand His will through His Word. Speaking to the Jews in the church at Rome, the Apostle Paul wrote:

> **Behold, thou art called a Jew, and restest in the law, and makest thy boast of God, AND KNOWEST HIS WILL, and approvest the things that are more**

excellent, BEING INSTRUCTED OUT OF THE LAW. (Capital letters added for emphasis.)

The Jews were said to know God's will because they were instructed out of the law, or Torah. The law, or Torah, taught them how they were to live their lives acceptably before God. It teaches us what to do and what not to do. By the law or Torah is the knowledge of sin (Rom. 3: 20), and the knowledge of how to live a holy life. Every believer should also know God's will as we are instructed to study to show ourselves approved unto Him; workmen that do not need to be ashamed, rightly dividing the Word of truth (2 Tim. 2:15).

God's Word also states, **"Wherefore be ye not unwise, but understanding what the will of the Lord is"** (Eph. 5:17). So those who do not understand God's will lack wisdom. God's people should be the wisest, most knowledgeable, and most understanding people on the earth as a result of learning His Word. Moses told Israel:

> **Behold, I have taught you statutes and judgments, even as the LORD my God commanded me, that ye should do so in the land whither ye go to possess it. Keep therefore and do them; for this is your wisdom and your understanding in the sight of the nations, which shall hear all these statutes, and say, Surely this great nation is a wise and understanding people** (Deut. 4:5-6).

Knowing God's Will Through His Spirit

Under the New Covenant we also have the indwelling of God's Spirit, which teaches us all things, and brings God's Word to our remembrance (Jn. 14:26). God's Spirit also guides us into all truth, shows us things to come, and reveals to us the things that God has given to us in Christ (Jn. 16:13-15).

The scriptures also teaches that God's Spirit reveals to us the things which God has prepared for them that love Him, and the things that are freely given to us by Him. (1 Cor. 2:9-12).

Under the inspiration of the Holy Spirit, Paul prayed that those of the Colossian church (which would also apply to us) might be filled with the knowledge of God's will in all wisdom and spiritual understanding. This was for the purpose of walking worthy of the Lord unto all pleasing, to be fruitful in every good work, and to continue to increase in the knowledge of God (Col. 1:9-10).

Coming to know God's will is really not all that big of a task. One must just spend time with Him by studying His Word and praying. Our relationship with God is the same kind of a relationship that a child has with their natural father. A child quickly learns the will of his/her father by spending time with him. At a relatively young age most children learn what their fathers will give them and what he will not, even before they ask him. This comes from spending time with him and learning about him. That is the kind of relationship we are to develop with God. Scripture does make it clear that we are to know what God's will is when we pray. 1 John 5:14-15 states:

> **And this is the confidence that we have in him, that, if we ask any thing according to his will, he heareth us: And if we know that he hear us, whatsoever we ask, we can know that we have the petitions that we desired of Him.**

Most people relate to God as their Father in the same way they relate to their earthly father. So, you need to examine your relationship with you earthly father to see if it is affecting your relationship with your heavenly Father.

Jesus Christ as Our Example

As always, the life of Jesus is our example to follow. Remember, He was born into this world as a baby and grew up into a man. He could not have possibly known who He was at birth, or God's will for His life. These are things that God must have revealed to Him through the scriptures. He had to learn God's will for His life. He clearly came to know what His Father's (God) will was in general, and for His life. He told His disciples, "**My meat is to do the will of him that sent me, and to finish his work**" (Jn. 4:34). He also stated, "**For I came down from heaven, not to do mine own will, but the will of him that sent me**" (Jn. 6:38). This should be the attitude of each and every believer. We should study God's Word to find out what His will is, and what He has called each of us to do.

Those who do not come to know God's will have little desire to know Him, or to live a holy life. Romans 12:1-2 states:

> **I beseech you therefore, brethren, by the mercies of God, that ye present your bodies a living sacrifice, holy, acceptable unto God, which is your reasonable service. And be not conformed to this world: but be ye transformed by the renewing of your mind, that ye may prove what is that good, and acceptable, and perfect, will of God.**

The knowledge of God's will therefore comes by the renewing of our minds. This takes place through the effectual working of God's Word in those that believe (1 Thess. 2:13).

Chapter 17

ACCORDING TO YOUR FAITH BE IT UNTO YOU

The gospel of Matthew records an account of two blind men that followed Jesus, crying, and saying, "Thou Son of David, have mercy on us." When they came into the house where He was, Jesus asked them, "Believe ye that I am able to do this." They said unto Him, "Yea, Lord." Jesus then touched their eyes, and said, **"According to your faith be it unto you"** (Matt. 9:27-29). According to this statement we can receive from God whatever we have the faith to believe Him for. This makes faith extremely important in every believer's life. These two men had the faith to receive their sight.

There are some important lessons that we can learn from these two men. First, they followed Jesus and diligently sought Him out, not letting their blindness stand in their way. Second, they recognized Jesus for who He is. Calling Him the Son of David was their recognition of Him as the Messiah as He was to come through the lineage of David. Third, they believed that He was able to perform what was written in God's Word concerning Him. These three things are all building blocks to faith. We must follow and seek after God, we must believe that He is what He says He is, and that He will perform His Word in our lives. Hebrews 11:6 states, **"But without faith it is impossible to please him:**

for he that cometh to God must believe that he is, and that he is a rewarder of them that diligently seek him".

Great Faith or Little Faith

Jesus often spoke of men as having either great faith or little faith. He was pleased with those of great faith, and displeased and unbraided those with little faith. The little faith of the majority was a disappointment to Him. This means that every believer can and should obtain great faith. Of course this does not just happen overnight, but our faith should steadily increase as we grow and mature in Christ.

It is surprising to find how many Christians have little faith, and a poor understanding of what faith really is. Faith is what gives us the ability to believe God. Quoting from the Amplified bible, Hebrews 11:1 states:

> **Now faith is the assurance (the confirmation, the title deed) of the things [we] hope for, being the proof of things [we] do not see and the conviction of their reality [faith perceiving as real fact what is not revealed to the senses].**

Out of the King James, it simply states, "**Now faith is the substance of things hoped for, the evidence of things not seen.**" Substance is the essence or intrinsic properties of a thing. Evidence is the existence of something that is proof of a thing.

Faith leaves no room for doubt. James 1:5-7 states:

> **If any of you lack wisdom, let him ask of God, that giveth to all men liberally, and upbraideth not; and it shall be given him. But let him ask in faith, nothing wavering. For he that wavereth is like a wave of the sea driven with the wind and tossed. For let not that man think that he shall receive any thing of the Lord.**

To have faith is to know that one will receive what he asks for. This comes as a result of knowing that what we ask for is according to God's will for us to have. We learn God's will and obtain this kind of faith through His Word.

How to Obtain Great Faith

We will find that faith originates from God, and that God lives by faith. It is a part of His nature. He cannot doubt nor have unbelief. This makes it impossible for Him to fail. His Word cannot return to him void, and will always accomplish and prosper in what He sends it to do (Isa. 55:11). This is because He speaks in absolute faith. He is the same yesterday, today and tomorrow.

So how do we obtain this faith? Scripture does make it clear that God's people are to live by faith. Romans 10:17 states, **"So then faith cometh by hearing, and hearing by the word of God."** God's Word is what produces faith in our lives and is also what causes it to grow. Anything believed in other than God's Word is not really faith. It is just a belief in something else. We will find that only God and His children actually live by faith. Those born of God have His Spirit, which is also essential for us to live by faith.

When speaking of the faith of the Old Testament saints, Habakkuk 2:4 states, **"Behold, his soul which is lifted up is not right in him: but the just shall live by his faith."** Whenever this scripture is quoted in the New Testament, it says, **"The just shall live by faith"** (Rom. 1:17, Gal. 3:11, Heb. 10:38). In every account in the New Testament the word 'his' is not found. It was left out for a very good reason. Remember, faith originates from God. The Old Testament saints, none of which were born of God's Spirit, lived by His (God's) faith as the Spirit moved in their lives. Under the New Covenant, that faith becomes ours as we are joined to God through the indwelling of His Spirit. We receive faith through God's Spirit who opens our ears to hear His Word. This is why faith is spoken of in reference to the fruit of the Spirit (Gal. 5:22), and is also one of the gifts of the Spirit (I Cor. 12:9). This is also why many passages of scripture speak of our faith as being BY CHRIST, or that we live by THE FAITH OF CHRIST (Acts 3:16, Gal. 2:16, 20, Phil. 3:9, 1 Pet. 1:21).

Faith is a living, active part of God's Spirit. The book of James tells us that faith without works is dead (Jas. 2:17, 20, 26). True faith is alive and active. The proof of our faith is the works it produces (Jas. 17-26). One cannot have faith without it producing an action (or work) in their life. This is seen from the moment of salvation as we are saved by grace through faith (Eph. 2:8). For example, when we hear the gospel of our salvation, and believe in our hearts, it produces the confession (work) of Jesus Christ with our mouths (Rom. 10:8-10).

Examples of Great Faith

Let's look at some examples of those that scripture speaks of as having great faith, the actions that faith produced in their lives, and the lessons we can learn to strengthen our faith. The gospel of Matthew tells of a woman of Canaan who came to Jesus pleading for Him to cast a devil out of her daughter. At first Jesus did not even answer her, and His disciples wanted Him to send her away. This was because she did not belong to Israel. When Jesus did answer her, He said, "**I am not sent but unto the lost sheep of the house of Israel.**" She then came and worshipped Him, saying, "**Lord, help me.**" Jesus then told her, "**It is not meat to take the children's bread, and to cast it to dogs.**" She did not get offended when Jesus more or less called her a dog (it was common for Jews to call Gentiles dogs), and said, "**Truth, Lord: yet the dogs eat of the crumbs which fall from their masters' table.**" Then Jesus said unto her, "**O woman, great is thy faith: be it unto thee even as thou wilt.**" Her daughter was made whole that very hour (Matt. 15:21-28). Great faith is persistent and insistent. As it is produced by hearing God's Word, and is the substance and evidence of the things hoped for and not seen. Faith will not take no for an answer. Faith is like a rope that is tied to the things we ask for, pulling them toward us until they arrive.

The gospel of Mark tells of four men that carried a man sick of the palsy to Jesus. As they could not reach Him because of the crowd, they climbed on the roof, broke through it, and lowered him down to Jesus. As a result of this action, the Word says that Jesus SAW THEIR FAITH, and the man with the palsy was forgiven and healed (Mk. 2:1-12). God will always see true faith by the works it produces. Scripture states, "**The eyes of the LORD run to and fro throughout the whole earth, to shew himself strong in behalf of them whose heart is perfect toward him**" **(2 Chr. 16:9).** These men went to whatever extremes were necessary to get into the presence of Jesus. That is what faith does for us. It overcomes all obstacles and brings us into the presence of God.

Mark chapter five shows us two people of great faith. First we have a man named Jairus, whose daughter was at the point of death. Jairus came to Jesus requesting that he go and lay His hands on his daughter so she would be healed. Jesus then proceeded to go with him. As he went, a multitude of people followed Him and crowded around Him. Then a woman, which had an issue of blood for twelve years, came up behind him and touched His garment. Jesus then asked who had touched Him. His disciples were at a loss at how to answer Him as a multitude of people were pressing against Him and touching Him. He was speaking of the one touch of faith that caused virtue (or power) to go out from Him. This woman had touched His clothes by faith, causing power to go out from Him, giving the woman her healing. Jesus attributed her healing entirely to her faith. Our faith is connected to the power of God. It is what draws His unlimited power from Him and brings it to us.

After this delay, there came a messenger informing Jairus that his daughter had died. When Jesus heard the word that was spoken, He said unto Jairus, "**Be not afraid, only believe.**" He then went and raised the twelve-year-old girl from the dead. There are some important points we need to see here. First, Jesus went with Jairus upon his request for Him to heal his daughter. The only reason that Jesus would go with him was to heal her. The fact that she died before Jesus got there did not change anything. To keep Jairus from doubting at the word of his daughter's death, Jesus said unto him, "Be not afraid, only believe." In the same way, we must believe God's Word regardless of any circumstances or events that would seem to keep it from coming to pass in our lives. Nothing can limit or keep God from performing His Word. Not even the death of what God's Word has promised us.

Abraham is a great example of this. God promised Abraham a son, and to make him the father of many nations. This took place when he was already seventy-five years old. God's Word then states, "**Abraham believed God, and it was counted unto him for righteousness**" (Rom. 4:3, Gen.,15:6). At that time Abraham's wife was barren, but he was still able to have children. However, twenty-four years later things had changed. Neither Abraham nor Sarah (his wife) was able to have children. Concerning this, Romans 4:17-21 states:

> **(As it is written, I have made thee a father of many nations,) before him whom he believed, even God, who quickeneth the dead, and calleth those things which be not as though they were. Who against hope believed in hope, that he might become the father of many nations; according to that which was spoken, So shall thy seed be. And being not weak in faith, he considered not his own body now dead, when he was about an hundred years old, neither yet the deadness of Sara's womb: He staggered not at the promise of God through unbelief; but was strong in faith, giving glory to God; And being fully persuaded that, what he had promised, he was able also to perform.**

Abraham had a supernatural hope when all natural hope was gone. When there was nothing left in the world, or of the flesh to have hope in, he still had hope in the promise that God made to him. He did not CONSIDER that his body was dead or the deadness of Sarah's womb. These things did not cause his faith to stagger or waver. He had become fully persuaded that God was going to bring His promises to pass regardless of these circumstances, which He did. God brings life out of death. Many of His promises to us must first die before God brings them forth in our lives. We must also have faith like Abraham. God's Word must become more real unto us than anything we see, hear, smell, taste or touch with our natural senses. Scripture goes on to say:

> **And therefore it was imputed to him for righteousness. Now it was not written for his sake alone, that it was imputed to him; But for us also, to whom it shall be imputed, if we believe on him that raised up Jesus our Lord from the dead** (Rom. 4:22-24).

The gospel of Luke tells us of a centurion that had a servant that was sick and ready to die. As he was not of Israel, the elders of Israel spoke to Jesus on his behalf as this man loved Israel and had built them a synagogue. As Jesus was on the way to the centurion's house, the centurion sent a friend, saying:

> **Lord, trouble not thyself: for I am not worthy that thou shouldest enter under my roof: Wherefore neither thought I myself worthy to come unto thee: but say in a word, and my servant shall be healed. For I also am a man set under authority, having under me soldiers, and I say unto one, Go, and he goeth; and to another, Come; and he cometh; and to my servant, Do this, and he doeth it. When Jesus heard these things, he marveled at him, and turned him about, and said unto the people that followed him, I say unto you, I have not found so great faith, no, not in Israel** (Lk. 7:1-10).

What made this man's faith so great? He had faith in the Word sent by Jesus as he understood that Jesus came and spoke under the authority of God. Caesar, the highest authority in the Roman Empire, set this man in a position of authority. He carried out the word of Caesar without question, as those under his command carried out his word. He did not have to be present for a word sent by him to be carried out. It would lose no power. He understood the power of the Word sent by Jesus, who came under the authority of God. In the same way, we need to understand the power of God's Word, the highest authority in the universe. This will give us this same kind of faith in the Word (the bible) that God has sent us. The only thing that will hinder God's Word from coming to pass in our lives is our lack of faith.

Chapter 18

ABIDING IN CHRIST

The bible often uses the word 'abide' concerning our state and relationship with Christ. The word abide means to 'stay or live in a given place, state, relationship or expectancy.' To abide in Christ is to abide in God's Word, His love, His light, and His righteousness. It is to dwell in a place of safety and protection from all things that might come upon or against us (Ps. 91:1-13).

As a natural law, each one of us abides somewhere. If we do not abide in the light of Christ we abide in the darkness of the world (Jn. 12:46). We will either abide in belief or unbelief (Rom. 11:23). Where we abide depends upon whether or not we have been born again. If we have been born again we do abide in Christ, and He in us (Jn. 14:20). However, to what extent we abide in Christ depends upon how much we live for Christ, and how much He lives through us as a result of our obedience.

Manifested by Love and Obedience

Christ abides in us, and we in Him, through the indwelling of the Holy Spirit. This is manifested by our love for God, which is manifested by our obedience to God's Word. Keeping His commandments is the proof of our love for God, and our abiding in Christ. Jesus told His disciples:

> **If ye love me, keep my commandments. And I will pray the Father, and he shall give you another Comforter, that he may abide with you forever; Even the Spirit of truth; whom the world cannot receive, because it seeth him not, neither knoweth him: but ye know him; for he dwelleth with you, and shall be in you. I will not leave you comfortless: I will come to you** (Jn. 14:15-18). He also stated, **If a man love me, he will keep my words: and my Father will love him, and we will come unto him, and make our abode with him"** (Jn. 14:23).

Not nearly everyone who claims to abide in Christ actually does. According to scripture, those who do not keep God's Word (commandments) do not love Him or abide in Christ. We can therefore measure our love for God, and how much we really abide in Christ, by how obedient we are to keeping His Word. The real proof that we abide in Him is that we keep His word, and walk as He walked (1 Jn. 2:3-6). Jesus also stated that if we keep His commandments, we would abide in His love, even as He had kept His Father's commandments, and abode in His love (Jn. 15:10).

Manifested by a Love for God's Children

Those who abide in Christ are also manifested by their love for God's children. 1 Jn. 2:9-11 states:

> **He that saith he is in the light, and hateth his brother, is in darkness even until now. He that loveth his brother abideth in the light, and there is none occasion of stumbling in him. But he that hateth his brother is in darkness, and walketh in darkness, and knoweth not whither he goeth, because that darkness hath blinded his eyes.**

One cannot be born of God's Spirit and hate another that is also born of God's Spirit. Christ abiding in one believer will automatically love Christ abiding in every other believer. Hatred is a manifestation of the spirit of the enemy hating the Spirit of God. Everyone that loves God will also love those that are born of God (1 Jn. 4:20-5:3).

Manifested by Our Fruit

Another manifestation that one abides in Christ is the fruit they bear. Jesus stated in Jn. 15:4-5:

> **Abide in me, and I in you. As the branch cannot bear fruit of itself, except it abide in the vine; no more can ye, except ye abide in me. I am the vine, ye are the branches: He that abideth in me, and I in him, the same bringeth forth much fruit: for without me ye can do nothing.**

The fruit a person bears is how we know those who are saved, and those who are not (Matt. 7:15-20). The fruit that each true believer should bear is the fruit of the Spirit. Galatians 5:22 tell us that this fruit is love, joy, peace, longsuffering, gentleness, goodness, faith, meekness, and temperance. These are the things that we should look for in the lives of believers.

Has No Commitment to Sin

Those who abide in Christ are also kept from sin. 1 Jn. 3:6 states, **"Whosoever abideth in him sinneth not: whosoever sinneth hath not seen him, neither knoweth him."** Of course this does not speak of being without sin, but of those who continue to abide in what they know to be sin. Those who abide in Christ will endeavor to live a righteous life. They will not have a commitment to sin. Those who abide in Christ will feel the need to repent of any sin and continue to go forward in their relationship with God.

In the Old Testament, the tabernacle of Moses and the temples of the Lord were types of the body or church of Jesus Christ. The Word teaches us that those who abide in God's tabernacle are those who walk uprightly, work righteousness, speak truth in their hearts, do not backbite, or do evil to their neighbor, and in whose eyes a vile person is despised (Ps. 15:1-4).

Chapter 19

STRANGERS AND PILGRIMS

God's Word refers to believers as strangers and pilgrims as a reminder of who we really are, where we come from, where we belong, and why we so often feel out of place in this world. The biblical meaning of a stranger is one of another land, nation, family or tribe. A pilgrim is a foreigner or sojourner.

Born again believers are born of (from) God (Jn. 1:13, 1 Jn. 4:7, 5:1, 4, 18). This means that we are born from heaven, and shall bear the image of the heavenly (1 Cor. 15:47-49). Upon salvation we traded our earthly citizenship in for a heavenly one. Our citizenship is now in heaven (Phil. 2:20). This is why God's people have always felt out of place in this world. There is always that feeling we belong somewhere else.

Abraham, a Stranger Even in His Inheritance

We see a natural example of these things with Abraham. Genesis 12:1 states, **"Now the LORD had said unto Abram, Get thee out of thy country, and from thy kindred, and from thy father's house, unto a land that I will shew thee."**

Abram, whose name was later changed to Abraham, was told to leave his country, kindred, and family to go unto a land that God was to show him. This was the land of Canaan, which was spoken of as a land that flowed with milk and honey. It was a type of the kingdom of God, which abundantly supplies all the needs of God's people. Abraham traded his country in for a different one where God was to make of him a great nation. His descendants born in the land would be his kindred and family.

This is a type of what takes place in our lives upon salvation. We are chosen and delivered out of this world, and translated into the kingdom of God (Jn. 15:19, Gal. 1:4, Col. 1:13). We become a member of the family of God and those who are also born of God become our fathers, mothers, sisters and brothers. Jesus gave us an example of this as He was talking to the people one day. He was informed that His mother and brethren stood without, desiring to speak to him.

> **But he answered and said unto him that told him, Who is my mother? and who are my brethren? And he stretched forth his hand toward his disciples, and said, Behold my mother and my brethren! For whosoever shall do the will of my Father which is in heaven, the same is my brethren, and sister, and mother** (Matt. 12:48-50).

Even our relationships with unsaved family members might drastically change after salvation. When a person is truly saved, it will change the way they live their life. This can seem very strange to those who we were close to before salvation. Ps. 69:8 states, **"I am become a stranger unto my brethren, and an alien unto my mother's children."**

God then promised to give Abraham and his descendants that land, which was then inhabited by the Canaanites (Gen. 12:6, 13:15-16). The bible even speaks of him as being a stranger in that land (Gen. 17:8).

This is a type of God's children being heirs to all things, but not yet possessing all things.

God also told Abraham:

> **Know of a surety that thy seed shall be a stranger in a land that is not theirs, and shall serve them; and they shall afflict them four hundred years; And also that nation, whom they shall serve, will I judge: and afterward shall they come out with great substance** (Gen. 15:13-14).

The nation they served was Egypt, which is a type of the world. This is a type or shadow of us living as foreigners and sojourners in this world after salvation. There is also an appointed time when God shall judge the world and bring His people out with great substance.

As Abraham was a stranger in the land that he and his descendants were to inherit, he still felt out of place. As the land of Canaan is only a type of the kingdom of God, Abraham knew that there had to be more than just an earthly inheritance. Hebrews 11:8-10 states:

> **By faith Abraham, when he was called to go out into a place which he should after receive for an inheritance, obeyed; and he went out, not knowing whither he went. By faith he sojourned in the land of promise, as in a strange country, dwelling in tabernacles with Isaac and Jacob, the heirs with him of the same promise: For he looked for a city which hath foundations, whose builder and maker is God.**

By faith Abraham actually looked for a city that was built by God. This could be none other than the holy city, the New Jerusalem, which will come down from God out of heaven. We read about this city in the twenty-first chapter of the book of Revelation. Speaking of the people of great faith in the Old Testament, Hebrews 11:13-16 goes on to say:

> These all died in faith, not having received the promises, but having seen them afar off, and were persuaded of them, and embraced them, and confessed that they were strangers and pilgrims on the earth. For they that say such things declare plainly that they seek a country. And truly, if they had been mindful of that country from which they came out, they might have had opportunity to have returned. But now they desire a better country, that is, an heavenly: wherefore God is not ashamed to be called their God: for he hath prepared for them a city.

Even after Israel received the land of their inheritance, they were told they could not sell it for the land was actually God's, and they were strangers and sojourners with Him (Lev. 25:23). That is the way we are to live our lives on this earth, as strangers and sojourners with God.

King David

King David must have felt much the same way. He stated, **"I am a stranger in the earth: hide not thy commandments from me"** (Ps. 119:19). God's commandments are to teach us how to live in our heavenly inheritance as we sojourn here on earth. After giving generously for the building of God's temple, King David also stated:

> But who am I, and what is my people, that we should be able to offer so willingly after this sort? for all things come of thee, and of thine own have we given thee. For we are strangers before thee, and sojourners, as were all our fathers: our days on the earth are as a shadow, and there is none abiding.

We are truly strangers and pilgrims here on this earth. However, salvation does not change the fact that we are still wrapped up in this sinful body of flesh. God's Word therefore tells us, **"Dearly beloved,**

I beseech you as strangers and pilgrims, abstain from fleshly lusts, which war against the soul" (1 Pet. 2:11-12). The flesh is that which is born of this world, and is in agreement with it. Upon salvation we enter into warfare between the flesh and the Spirit. The flesh and the Spirit are contrary one to the other (Gal. 5:17). The soul is the battlefield. As we are no longer of the flesh, or of this world, we are to abstain from the lusts of the flesh that cause this war to rage on.

As we grow and mature in Christ, the world actually becomes strange to us, and we to the world. 1 Peter 4:3-4 states:

> **For the time past of our life may suffice us to have wrought the will of the Gentiles, when we walked in lasciviousness, lusts, excess of wine, revellings, banqueting, and abominable idolatries: Wherein they think it strange that ye run not with them to the same excess of riot, speaking evil of you.**

Chapter 20

GOING THROUGH (WATER AND FIRE)

"When thou passest through the waters, I will be with thee; and through the rivers, they shall not overflow thee: when thou walkest through the fire, thou shalt not be burned; neither shall the flame kindle upon thee" (Isaiah 43:2).

God's Word does not say IF you pass through the waters, or IF you walk through the fire, but WHEN. This is therefore something that will take place in the life of every believer.

However, we do have God's promise that he will be with us that the waters will not overflow and sweep us away, and the fire will not burn or kindle upon us.

Water and Fire Cleanse and Purify Our Lives

God does not cause us to go through anything that is not necessary and beneficial for our lives. It is essential for us to pass through the water and fire to be cleansed and purified. Num. 31:23 states:

> Everything that may abide the fire, ye shall make it go through the fire, and it shall be clean: nevertheless it shall be purified with the water of separation: and all that abideth not the fire ye shall make go through the water.

This scripture is in reference to the spoil, which included human captives, that was taken by Israel in a war against Midian. The water of separation symbolizes the purification from the defilement of sin and death, which was provided through the blood of Christ for every believer. Nevertheless, EVERYTHING that may abide the fire has to go through the fire to be clean, and that which cannot abide the fire must go through the water. That which may abide the fire is the gold, silver, brass and other metals. This is important because the bible often refers to believers as being silver and gold that is refined and purified by going through the fire (Zech. 13:9, Mal. 3:2-3, Isa. 1:25).

What is it to Pass Through Water and Fire?

So what is God's Word referring to when it speaks of us passing through water and fire? Let's look at Psalms 66:10-12, which states:

> For thou, O God, hast proved us: thou hast tried us, as silver is tried. Thou hast broughtest us into the net; thou hast laidst affliction upon our loins. Thou hast caused men to ride over our heads; we went through fire and through water: but thou broughtest us out into a wealthy place.

God's Word teaches that we are tried and proven through affliction. These afflictions include the attacks of the enemy that come against us, and are often spoken of as going through the fire and water. For example, the Assyrian army is spoken of as the waters of the river that overflowed its banks, and was poured out into Judah (Isa. 8:6-8). Even the attacks of the enemy are designed to cleanse, purge, and bring forth deliverance in our lives.

Going Through the Fire

An excellent example of going through the fire is found in the third chapter of the book of Daniel. This is the well-known story of Shadrach, Meshach and Abednego. As a result of refusing to worship a golden image set up by Nebuchadnezzar the king of Babylon, these three Hebrew men were cast into a burning fiery furnace. Because of Nebuchadnezzar's rage at their refusal, he commanded the furnace to be heated up seven times hotter than usual; and then commanded the mightiest men in his army to cast them into the furnace. These three men were then bound and cast into a fire so hot that it actually killed the mighty men who cast them in. When Nebuchadnezzar then looked into the fire, he did not see three bound men being consumed by the fire, but four loose men walking in the midst of it. The fire had consumed their bands but had no power upon their bodies. Not a single hair on their heads was singed, their coats were not damaged, nor had the smell of the fire passed on them. What a demonstration of what God had spoken to the prophet Isaiah (43:2). These three Hebrew men actually walked through the fire, and according to God's promise, He was right there with them. He only could have been the fourth man that Nebuchadnezzar saw walking in the fire. After they came forth from the midst of the fire, they were free from serving any other god, and were promoted in the province of Babylon. This deliverance and freedom was only granted and experienced by those who went through the fire.

This is a natural example of what takes place spiritually in our lives. After salvation we can still be bound by certain sins, demonic strongholds, and yet love and (ignorantly) worship the things (gods) of this world. It is therefore essential that we go through the fire to be cleansed and loosed from that which has us bound. The mighty men that were slain when they cast the three Hebrew men into the fire are symbolic of the sins and strongholds that cause it to be necessary for us to go through the fire. The fire is designed to burn up the very things that bring us to it, as well as all that has us bound. The fire is symbolic of the trials, sufferings, and afflictions that Christians are appointed to (1 Pet. 4:12-13, Phil. 1:29, 1 Thess. 3:3-5).

It is also important to consider that these three Hebrew men knew the consequence of not worshipping the image was to be cast into the fiery furnace, and they refused anyway. There were most certainly other Jews there that did fall down and worship the image to avoid being cast into the furnace. These three could have also compromised and fell down and worshipped the image, but chose the fire instead. Although our decisions may not be a matter of life and death, each of us must make these types of decisions during our Christian walk. Some things we must endure are out of our control, but others are not. It is sad that so many choose to compromise rather than live the godly lifestyle that will cause them to suffer persecution (2 Tim. 3:12); or go through the trials and afflictions that purify our faith and bring spiritual growth (Jas. 1:2-4, 1 Pet. 1:7). Many of us do not really experience God because we do everything we can not to go through any hardship as children of God. God meets us in the fire (or water) that we go through because of our faith. That is where we are loosed from the things that have us bound. We experience true freedom on the other side of the fiery furnace and rivers of waters. The only way to get there is to go through.

It is also interesting to note that water and fire are both symbolic of the Holy Spirit, and His work in our lives. Jesus often used the example of water to teach about the Holy Spirit (Matt. 3:11, Jn. 4:6-15, 7:37-39). The baptism with the Holy spirit is also to come with fire to purge his people, and burn up the chaff with unquenchable fire (Matt. 3:12, Acts 2:3).

Going Through the Water

Once again, God gives us a natural example with the nation of Israel. After delivering them out of Egypt, God led them to a place called

Pihahiroth (see Ex. 14). It was a place where the Red sea was before them, and mountains on both sides. God then hardened Pharaoh's heart that he would pursue and come up behind them. This was to complete their deliverance from Egypt. God divided the Red sea so his people could walk across on dry ground, but then caused the sea to come together and drown the Egyptians who tried to pursue after them. This was done for Israel to see the salvation of the Lord, and that the Egyptians whom they had served they would see again no more (Ex. 14:13).

Going through the Red sea was a baptism for the nation of Israel (1 Cor. 10:1-2). It was also the place where the hold that Pharaoh (a type of Satan) and Egypt (a type of the world) had over them was destroyed once and for all. Our baptism into Christ by God's Spirit is what destroys the works of the devil in our lives, and delivers us from this present evil world (1 Cor. 12:13, 1 Jn. 3:8, Gal. 1:4). Even though we still go through difficult times, nothing we face has the power to destroy us. We are only made better as we are cleansed and purified from all ungodliness.

Chapter 21

AFFLICTIONS, PERSECUTIONS, TRIALS AND TRIBULATIONS

Salvation does not bring an end to all of life's difficulties by any means. Actually, believers are appointed to go through afflictions, persecutions, trials and tribulations; with each of these things necessary in our lives.

The Purpose of Afflictions

God uses afflictions to prepare us for salvation, cleanse and purge our lives after we are saved, bring us back after having gone astray, and to bring forth spiritual growth in our lives. It is no wonder that scripture states:

> **Many are the afflictions of the righteous: but the LORD delivereth him out of them all** (Ps. 34:19). 1 Thess. 3:3 also says, **That no man should be moved by these afflictions: for yourselves know that we are appointed thereunto.**

He that does the appointing can be none other than God Himself. Psalms 119:75 also states, **"I know, O LORD, that thy judgments are right, and that thou in faithfulness hast afflicted me."**

Few, if any, ever come to salvation when everything is running smoothly in their lives. It is a time of affliction that brings one to the end of him or herself, and causes one to realize his need for God.

Before there ever was a nation of Israel, God informed Abraham that his seed would be afflicted in a land that was not theirs for 400 years (Gen. 15: 13). The worst of this affliction took place during the time they were in bondage to Egypt. This affliction was absolutely necessary because Israel had become comfortable and content in the land of Egypt, with no real reason for them to leave. The Word states that God actually turned the hearts of the Egyptians to hate His people and to put them in bondage (Ps. 105:25). This affliction is what caused them to lose their desire and affection for Egypt, and look to the Promised Land. It was because of the affliction of this bondage that Israel looked unto God and cried out for deliverance (Ex. 2:23-25, 3:7-8).

The way God delivered Israel out of the land of Egypt is a shadow and type of the way that He works salvation to the inhabitants of the earth. God's Word often speaks of Egypt as the iron furnace that God delivered His people from (Deut. 4:20, 1 Ki. 8:51, Jer. 11:4). The book of Isaiah states that God chose them in the furnace of affliction (Isa. 48:10). When Israel cried out to God by reason of the bondage (Ex. 2:23), God looked upon their affliction, and sent them a savior (Moses) to deliver them from Egypt (a type of the world), and destroy the hold that Pharaoh (a type of Satan) had over them. This all pointed to Jesus Christ, the true Savior, who delivers us from this present evil world, and destroys the works of the devil in our lives (Gal. 4:4, 1 Jn. 3:8).

Those who live comfortable and basically trouble free in the world seldom, if ever, realize their need for God, and have no reason to call upon His name. They remain unaware that they are servants unto sin (Jn. 8:34), and are held captive by Satan, the god of this world (2 Cor. 4:4).

God also uses afflictions to bring us back to Him after we have gone astray. Psalms 119:67 & 71 states, **"Before I was afflicted I went astray: but now have I kept thy word. It is good for me that I have been afflicted; that I might learn thy statutes."** We have the tendency to seek God in times of affliction, but become spiritually slothful when all is going well. It is easy to pray and search the scriptures when we are in need of God to do something in our lives, but just as easy to neglect these spiritual duties when all is going well. Afflictions cause us to keep our eyes upon God and are a constant reminder of our need for Him.

Afflictions are also designed to bring forth growth in the spiritual man. The Egyptian bondage not only caused Israel to look to God and cry out for deliverance, but also caused them to multiply and grow. Ex. 1:11 states, **"But the more they afflicted them, the more they multiplied and grew."** Afflictions help us to grow spiritually as they put us in a position where we must seek God. If we do not seek God will all our hearts, and all of our souls, we will never truly find Him (Deut. 4:29, Jer. 29:13-14). It's just not a common thing for us to seek God in this way without a time of affliction. However, when we turn to God in our trouble, and seek Him, we will find Him (2 Chr. 15:4).

The Purpose of Persecution

Persecution is also a part of the life of every believer. The amount of persecution we experience actually depends upon how godly of a life each of us live. 2 Tim. 3:12 states, **"Yea, and all that will live godly in Christ Jesus shall suffer persecution."** Godly living IN CHRIST JESUS brings persecution as it causes us to be hated by those who live ungodly lifestyles, or reject Jesus Christ as Savior. This means that we can actually judge how godly of a lifestyle we are living by the amount of persecution we receive. We receive persecution from unbelievers, those of other religions, those who claim to be Christians, and even true Christians who live carnal lifestyles.

Most persecution comes as a result of the spiritual hatred between God's Spirit and the spirit of Satan. Scripture teaches that there are two types of people on the earth: the children of God, and the children of the devil (1 Jn. 3:10). Those born (again) of God have God's Spirit. Those who are not born of God's Spirit are children of the devil regardless of their religion. They are born only of the flesh and have the same spirit and nature of the devil (Jn. 3:6, Eph. 1:2-3, Jn. 8:44). The results of this are a conflict and perpetual hatred between the flesh and the Spirit (Gal. 5:17). This is seen with the Old Testament examples of Ishmael and Isaac, and Jacob and Esau.

The Example of Ishmael and Isaac

Ishmael and Isaac were brothers, both born from Abraham. Ishmael was born first from an Egyptian bondwoman named Hagar. Isaac was born later from Sarah, Abraham's wife. The story of their births teaches us an important message. Let's start from the beginning. God promised Abraham a son when he was already seventy-five years old (Gen. 15:1-6). Ten years later, thinking that God had withheld his wife Sarah from having children, Abraham took her servant Hagar and had a child by her. Hagar bore a son whom they named Ishmael (Gen. 16). However, this was not the son that God had promised him. The promised son was to be born from Sarah his wife. Sarah then later conceived and bore Isaac (Gen. 17). Because Abraham acted on his own to have a son by the Egyptian bondwoman, the bible declares that Ishmael was born after the flesh. As Isaac was the son of promise, he is a type of Christ (God's Word), and declared to be born after the Spirit (Gal. 4:22-29). Gal.4:29 states, **"But as then he that was born after the flesh persecuted him that was born after the Spirit, even so it is now"**. It is a spiritual principle that those born after the flesh persecute those born after the Spirit.

The nation of Israel sprang from Isaac, and many of the Arabian nations sprang from Ishmael. The descendants of Ishmael are predominantly of the Muslim or Islamic religion. They are of those who surround and dwell in the presence of Israel, and persecute them until this day (Gen. 16:12). The main agenda of these Muslim nations is to destroy the nation of Israel altogether. They also have a perpetual hatred for Christians. This is a result of the spiritual battle that takes place between God and the satanic forces that fight against Him. Satan's main purpose is to destroy God's people. It is therefore the spirit of Satan that is the main influence behind the Muslim religion. Even an American Muslim has been quoted, saying, 'I hate Jews and Christians, and I don't know why.' Outwardly, this man realized that there was no real reason for him to hate Jews and Christians, he just knew that he did. He hated them because he was under the influence of the satanic spirit behind the Muslim religion.

The example of Esau and Jacob

The other example is that of Esau and Jacob. Esau is also a type of the flesh, and Jacob (God's chosen) is a type of the Spirit (Rom. 9:11-13). The anger and wrath that Esau had for Jacob did not die with him but passed down to his descendants. Esau's descendants had a perpetual anger, wrath, and hatred against the descendants of Jacob who made up the nation of Israel, and persecuted them from generation to generation (Obed. 10-14, Amos 1:11).

Persecution From Within

It is also surprising to realize how much persecution comes from those of the church, or those who claim to be. For example, look at the nation of Israel. The way God set up the nation of Israel in the natural (flesh) is a picture of the way He set up the church in the spirit. Those of surrounding nations seldom persecuted the prophets. Their main persecution came from those within Israel. The scriptures make it very clear that the nation of Israel is God's chosen people, but only a remnant of those in the nation make up God's actual elect (Rom. 9:6, 11:1-7). It was of those who were not the elect that severely persecuted and often killed the prophets. Jesus even stated in Matt. 5:10-12:

> **Blessed are they which are persecuted for righteousness' sake: for theirs is the kingdom of heaven. Blessed are ye, when men shall revile you, and persecute you, and shall say all manner of evil against you falsely, for my sake. Rejoice, and be exceeding glad: for great is your reward in heaven: for so persecuted they the prophets which were before you.**

Concerning the church, not nearly all who claim to be Christians really are. In the same way that only a remnant of those of Israel was (and is) actually the elect, only a remnant of those who claim to be Christians truly are. Most just hold the title of being a Christian, but have no real idea of what it is to be truly born of God's Spirit. For instance, our adversary has been very successful in convincing many that we do not need to be baptized with God's Spirit. Scripture teaches that we are ALL baptized into the Body of Christ by God's Spirit (1 Cor. 12:13), and those baptized into Christ are those who make up the true church. Contrary to the way many believe, scripture teaches that to be born again is to be baptized with the Holy Spirit. One cannot receive God's Spirit in any other way. Many denominations reject the biblical experience of being baptized with the Holy Spirit, and persecute those who are. This is a prime example of the flesh persecuting the Spirit. It is also surprising to find just how many people become immediately defensive or offended when they are informed that the baptism with the Holy Spiritt is THE PROMISE (of salvation) of God to every believer, and they need to receive Him according to the pattern given to us in God's Word (Acts 2:1-4, 10:44-48, 19:1-6). It would seem that every true believer would want everything that God has for him or her, especially the things concerning His Spirit. However, many have their eyes blinded by the god of this world (Satan, 2 Cor. 4:4). They hold firmly to what is taught by their denomination and explain away the things written in God's Word that oppose their doctrine.

There are also those who are truly saved but walk in carnality. This is to walk according to the flesh (which persecutes the Spirit). These do not like to be judged concerning their carnal walk, and will often persecute those who bring a word of correction to them. This is also an example of the way Israel persecuted the prophets sent to correct them. This has gotten so bad that the most commonly quoted scripture is no longer John 3:16 but Matthew 7:1, which states, **"Judge not, that ye be not judged."**

Persecution Spreads the Gospel and Brings Growth to the Church

However, as affliction brings forth growth in the spiritual man, persecution furthers the gospel and brings forth growth to the church. The book of Acts speaks of a great persecution that came against the church at Jerusalem, which caused many members of the church to be scattered abroad (Acts 8:1-3). Acts 8:4 then states, **"Therefore they that were scattered abroad went everywhere preaching the word."** The apostle Paul, who was heavily persecuted, stated, **"the things which happened unto me have fallen out rather for the furtherance of the gospel"** (Phil. 1:12). Paul stated this when he was a prisoner in Rome as a result of the persecution he received from the Jewish people. He also stated that there were some who were then preaching Christ, not sincerely, but supposing to add affliction to his bonds. This caused him to rejoice for the simple fact that Christ was being preached (Phil. 1:13-18).

Persecution also brings attention to the church, which brings attention to the gospel of Jesus Christ. Much persecution is against the gospel, which actually causes the message of the gospel to be proclaimed. When those of the church endure persecution, it causes others to take notice and examine the message of the gospel. In this we also need to rejoice. By God's wisdom, persecution helps the message of the gospel to be spread throughout the world.

The Purpose of Trials and Temptations

Trials and temptations also serve an important purpose in our lives. The book of James tells us to count it all joy when we fall into divers temptations, as the trying of our faith works patience. We are to then let patience have her perfect work that we may be mature and complete, wanting nothing (Jas. 1:2-4).

Temptations Try Our Faith

Temptations are what try our faith. Peter compares the trial of our faith to the fire that purifies gold, that our faith might be found unto praise, honour and glory at the appearing of Jesus Christ (1 Pet. 1:6-7). An untried faith is an untested faith. The words tried and tested are interchangeable. An untried faith is an impure faith that is subject to waiver (Jas. 1:5).

The Trying of Abraham's Faith

As always, God's Word gives us some excellent examples. First we have Abraham, the man scripture declares to be the father of faith. However, Abraham did not become the father of faith overnight. It took many years of trials and temptations as he walked with God. On two different occasions, in fear for his life, he lied about Sarah being his wife. He would never have feared for his life if his faith had not wavered concerning the promises that God had made to him. This caused Sarah to be taken by Pharaoh King of Egypt, and later by Abimelech King of Gerar in the land of the Philistines (Gen. 12:10-20, 20:1-18). God faithfully preserved her both times and delivered her back to Abraham untouched, and purged that fear out of his life.

Abraham also took Sarah's handmaid and had a son by her in his impatience to have the son that God had promised him. God rejected this son, named Ishmael, as he was not the son that God had promised to him. God then reassured Abraham of His promise. Thirteen years later Abraham had the faith not to stagger at God's promise (for a son) regardless of both his and Sarah's bodies being dead from old age (Rom. 4:18-21). After he patiently (which comes through the trying of our faith) endured he received the promise (Heb. 6:15).

The final test of Abraham's faith came through God's command for him to offer Isaac, the promised son, for a burnt offering. Gen. 22:1-2 states:

> **And it came to pass after these things, that God did tempt Abraham, and said unto him, Abraham: and he said, Behold, here I am. And he said, Take now thy son, thine only son Isaac, whom thou lovest, and get thee into the land of Moriah; and offer him there for a burnt-offering upon one of the mountains which I will tell thee of.**

God tempting (testing) Abraham does not contradict the New Testament passage of scripture that states that God does not tempt any man (Jas. 1:13-14). James is speaking of God not tempting any man with evil. As the trial of our faith is such an important matter, God will bring forth certain events that will try our faith (see also 2 Chr. 32:31). Abraham's obedience in his willingness to offer Isaac was proof of a tried and purified faith. The book of James also declares that this work of faith was the fulfillment of the scripture, which stated that Abraham believed God, and it was imputed unto him for righteousness (Gen. 15:6, Jas. 2:23).

The Trying of Job's Faith

Another example is Job. Job is known for the great trial of suffering and affliction he endured. Although he did not fully understand what was taking place in his life, or why, he did recognize that God was at work. Job 23:10 states, **"But he knoweth the way that I take: when he hath tried me, I shall come forth as gold."** The New Testament refers to the patience of Job. Remember, patience comes through the trial of our faith (Jas. 4:11). Hebrews states that we are all in need of patience, that after we have done the will of God, we might receive the promise (Heb. 10:36). As we are all in need of patience, we are also all in need of our faith to be tried.

Each of us should give heed to what took place in Job's life. Although we might not go through the same experience, we will all go through trials and tribulations. 1 Pet. 4:12 states, **"Beloved, think it not strange concerning the fiery trial which is to try you, as though some strange thing happened unto you."** We should also not think that there are certain temptations we will not experience (1 Cor. 10:13). We, as Job, should always be aware that no matter what we are experiencing or going through, God is always at work in our lives.

Chapter 22

GOD'S MIGHTY MEN

For ye see your calling, brethren, how that not many wise men after the flesh, not many mighty, not many noble, are called: But God hath chosen the foolish things of the world to confound the wise; and God hath chosen the weak things of the world to confound the things which are mighty; And base things of the world, and things which are despised, hath God chosen, yea, and things which are not, to bring to nought things that are: That no flesh should glory in his presence (1 Cor. 1:26-29).

God's mighty men are not who or what we would expect them to be, especially if we look at things from a worldly perspective. God does not choose men that are highly esteemed upon the earth. Actually, He will most often choose those that the world looks down upon, despises, or has rejected. This is to keep any person from taking the glory that God alone is worthy of receiving. Those with their own credentials will take the glory unto themselves rather than giving it unto God. They would believe that God chose and called them because of whom or what they are, and what they have to offer.

When we think of whom the bible calls mighty men, we most likely think of the mighty men who served with King David. As no other king of Israel had such mighty men, there was something special about the reign of King David and those who served with him.

David was the only king that defeated all the enemies of Israel, and established the kingdom of Israel as the most dominant kingdom of that time. That is what Christ will do at His second coming. He will conquer all the enemies of Israel, sit upon the throne of David, and rule over the nations of the earth from Jerusalem. King David's reign is a type of the reign of Christ. Those who served with David are therefore a type of those who now serve Jesus Christ.

There were those who served as soldiers in his army, there were captains of ten, captains of fifty, captains of a hundred, captains of a thousand, and those who the bible calls David's mighty men. The bible gives a list of their names (the mighty men), and tells of the great things that many of them accomplished as they fought against the enemies of Israel (2 Sam. 23:8-39, 1 Chr. 11:10-47). These men performed extraordinary things. So extraordinary that it is obviously impossible for any man to do such acts under his own power. As God fought for King David, those who fought for David did so by the power of God.

A study of God's Word reveals that many, if not all, of these mighty men joined David when he was yet running from King Saul. He had been anointed to be king by the prophet Samuel, but was not yet reigning over Israel. Those who came to him in the wilderness is a type of the foolish, weak, base, and despised that God has called and chosen to be in Christ; who has been anointed as King, but has not yet began His millennial reign on earth as King.

Speaking of those who came to David as he was running from Saul in the wilderness, 1 Sam. 22:2 states:

And every one that was in distress, and every one that was in debt, and every one that was discontented, gathered themselves unto him; and he became a captain over them: and there were with him about four hundred men.

These men recognized that David would someday reign as king over Israel, and joining him was the way out of their distress, debt, and discontentment. He would have the ability to free them. These are the exact type of people that come to Christ. Very few ever come to Jesus when everything is running smoothly in their lives. It is usually those who are in distress, realize the debt for sin we have no ability to pay, or are just discontent with the way things are going in their life. In any case, Jesus Christ is the way out. Jn. 8:36 states, **"If the Son therefore shall make you free, ye shall be free indeed."** As those who came to David in the wilderness found their place and later reigned with him in his kingdom, those who now come to Christ also find their place and will live and reign with Him in His kingdom.

The power that these men had is a natural example of the spiritual power that is available to us in Christ. God's power is manifested through Christ who dwells within each born again believer. God chooses those who are inadequate of themselves to show that the power and ability comes from Him. He chose Abraham, a childless man with a barren wife, to be the father of many nations. He chose Jacob, who lived up to his name, which means supplanter (Gen. 27:36), instead of his elder brother Esau. He chose Moses, who was not eloquent and slow of speech, to speak to Pharaoh and deliver His people out of Egypt. Rather than the religious leaders of that day He chose fisherman, a tax collector, and others of no reputation to be the apostles of Christ. He chose Peter to be the lead apostle who denied the Lord three times. He chose Saul (Paul), who heavily persecuted the church, to preach the faith that he once destroyed.

It does not matter what a person has done in the past, where a person comes from, how educated, strong or wealthy they are. God uses the foolish, weak, base, despised, and even those who are nothing in this world. God can take these and raise them up to be the mighty men of Jesus Christ. There is no one that God cannot use.

Chapter 23

OUR SPIRITUAL WARFARE

Every believer enters into a spiritual warfare upon salvation. We enter this warfare regardless of whether we know it, understand it, or want to. The bible calls us soldiers of Jesus Christ (2 Tim. 2:3-4). The purpose of a soldier is to fight a war. We can see this warfare fought throughout the pages of the bible beginning all the way back to the Garden of Eden with Adam and Eve.

Our Enemies Strategies

As God's chosen people, their enemies surrounded the nation of Israel on every side. The bible says that Satan takes unsaved men captive at his will (2 Tim. 2:25-26). The enemies who fought (and still do today) against Israel are unknowingly being used by Satan in an attempt to destroy God's people, and bring the purposes of God to naught. Nothing has really changed. Even today, an attack of the enemy that comes against those of the church can still come through men who hate, revile, and persecute God's people.

Every attack that comes against us is a spiritual attack. Many unsaved men, especially those of other religions, feel a hatred for God's people as a result of being of the same nature as the enemy. Eph. 2:2-3 states:

> **Wherein in time past** (before salvation) **ye walked according to the course of this world, according to the prince of the power of the air** (Satan)**, the spirit that NOW worketh in the children of disobedience** (those unsaved): **Among whom also we ALL had our conversation** (lifestyle) **in times past in the lusts of our flesh, fulfilling the desires of the flesh and of the mind; and were by NATURE the children of wrath, even as other**s. (Words in parenthesis and capitals added for emphasis.)

There are only two kinds of people on the earth: the children of God and the children of the devil (Jn. 8:44, 1 Jn. 3:8-10). One is either of the Spirit and nature of God, or of the spirit and nature of the devil. The two spirits are contrary and at enmity with one another.

The demonic influence behind many religions can put an hatred in the hearts of the people of those religions, causing them to hate God's people and reject Jesus Christ. Those of the Muslim (Islamic) religion have a hatred for Jews and Christians. It is in the heart of every Muslim nation in the Middle East to destroy the nation of Israel. They also have no love for America, which was established upon Christianity.

This is why the bible tells us that we do not fight against flesh and blood, but against principalities, against powers, against the rulers of the darkness of this world, against spiritual wickedness in high places (Eph. 6:12). This makes our warfare different from that of Israel under the Old Covenant because they did wrestle against flesh and blood. They had no power over demonic spirits, and therefore fought against the men who were under their influence. True believers today have the indwelling of God's Spirit, and through the Spirit have power over our entire enemy. Jesus stated, **"Behold, I give unto you power to tread on serpents and scorpions, and over all the power of the enemy: and nothing shall by any means hurt you" (Lk. 10: 19).** We have the same power to cast out devils that Jesus had, if only we can believe. We have the power to rebuke and stand against any demonic spirit in the name of Jesus. To stop the demonic spirit behind a spiritual attack will stop the attack, along with whatever instrument (a person or people, sickness, etc.) the enemy is using.

What Keeps Us From Victory

If a Spirit filled believer does not seem to possess the power of God's Spirit, it is due to either sin or a lack of faith. Sin separates a believer from God and stops the power of God from operating in their life (Isa. 59:2, Joshua 7:11-12). As our God is a God of faith, unbelief also stops God's power from operating in a believer's life (Matt. 17:14-20). To build our faith we must study God's Word, pray, fast, and keep sin out of our lives.

Another part of our spiritual warfare is against our flesh, or carnal nature. The bible often uses the term flesh when referring to the sinful fallen nature of man. The flesh is also contrary and wars against God's Spirit, and can be used by Satan to tempt us with evil. The bible instructs us to crucify the flesh (Gal. 5:24), make no provisions for it (Rom. 13:14), and mortify (put to death) the deeds of the body through the Spirit (Rom. 8:13). Any part of our fleshly carnal nature that we do not put to death will result in sin, and cause us to be defeated by our enemies. We mortify the deeds of our body through the Spirit by feeding the Spirit with God's Word, and starving the flesh by making no provisions for it. If we continue to feed our flesh with the things of the world such as ungodly movies or pornography (as examples), the flesh will remain strong. If we feed the flesh more than the Spirit, we will walk according to the flesh. The one we feed the most will be the strongest.

The importance of this is seen with the nation of Israel and the Canaanites that dwelt in the land of their inheritance. The Canaanites were a cursed race of people (Gen. 9:25), and are a type of our flesh that is already under condemnation, but not yet taken away. Upon salvation we are translated (placed) into the kingdom of Jesus Christ (Col. 1:13), which is our inheritance. As the Canaanites inhabited the land of Israel's inheritance, our flesh also inhabits the kingdom of Jesus Christ as we live this life after salvation. As God commanded Israel to utterly destroy (kill) all the Canaanites, we are also to put to death the sinful activity of the flesh.

God's command to the Israelites to utterly destroy all the Canaanites is confusing to many people as they were to kill not only the men, but also the women and children. God informed them that if they left any remain in the land, they would make them sin against Him, for they would eventually serve their gods (Ex. 23:31-33, Num. 33:52-55, Deut. 7:1-5). A study of the Old Testament clearly reveals that Israel did not utterly destroy the Canaanites as they were commanded, and did end up worshipping their gods. In the same way, if we do not utterly mortify our flesh, it will cause us to sin against God. We will always be drawn back into the world. To live according to the course of the world is to unknowingly worship Satan, the god of this world (2 Cor. 4:4). Any area of our flesh we do not utterly mortify will fight its way back (men), reproduce (women), and grow up in our lives (children).

Our spiritual warfare is nothing we should take lightly. We should all take to heart the words the Apostle Paul wrote to Timothy, and apply them to our lives:

> **Thou therefore endure hardness, as a good soldier of Jesus Christ. No man that warreth entangleth himself with the affairs of this life; that he may please him who hath chosen him to be a soldier** (2 Tim. 2:3-4).

Chapter 24

BE STRONG AND OF GOOD COURAGE

Be strong and of good courage were the words God spoke to both Moses and Joshua, which they also passed on to the people, as they prepared them to conquer the land of their inheritance. They were to have no fear as they went against seven nations greater and mightier that they were (Deut. 7:1).

Moses told the people, "**Be strong and of a good courage, fear not, nor be afraid of them: for the LORD thy God, he it is that doth go with thee; he will not fail thee, nor forsake thee**" (Deut. 31:6). Strength and courage comes as a result of possessing something greater and stronger than that which is to be overcome. God's people are to be strong and courageous. They are not to fear or be afraid of the enemies they face. The reason for this is clear; they have God on their side. God is with His people, goes before them, covers their back, fights for them, and makes their way prosperous. To fear is a lack of faith on our part.

Moses and Joshua as Types of Christ

After the death of Moses, Joshua led the people over the Jordan River to possess the land of their inheritance. Moses had prepared the people to enter into their inheritance, but died without crossing over the Jordan. This was for disobeying God's Word when he (Moses) was angry with the people. He later told the people of Israel that the Lord was wroth (wrathful, angry) with him for their sakes (Deut. 3:26). Moses is a type of Christ as He walked on the earth, and prepared the people to enter into God's Kingdom. He died on the cross as God's wrath and judgment came upon Him for our sakes. Joshua is a type of the resurrected Christ who brings us across into our inheritance as children of God.

Israel Crossing the Jordan is a Type of Salvation

The book of Joshua begins with God preparing Joshua to lead the people across the Jordan into the land He had promised them. Joshua 1:2-6 states:

> **Moses my servant is dead; now therefore arise, go over this Jordan, thou, and all this people, unto the land which I do give to them, even to the children of Israel. Every place that the sole of your foot shall tread upon, that have I given you, as I said unto Moses. From the wilderness and this Lebanon even unto the great river, the river Euphrates, all the land of the Hittites, and unto the great sea toward the going down of the sun, shall be your coast. There shall not any man be able to stand before thee all the days of thy life: as I was with Moses, so I will be with thee: I will not fail thee, nor forsake thee. Be strong and of a good courage: for unto this people shalt thou divide for an inheritance the land, which I sware unto their fathers to give them.**

The land of Canaan was promised to Abraham and his descendants well over four hundred years before this. It was a land that God GAVE unto them. Nevertheless, they still had to go to war with the people that then inhabited the land. They had to conquer the land in battle through the power of God. Their real warfare began when they entered into the land of their inheritance.

Crossing over the Jordan River into their inheritance is a type of our salvation. Our spiritual warfare begins at salvation when we cross over into the kingdom of God's Son (Col. 1:13). Just as the land of Canaan was given to Israel, our salvation is a gift from God. **"For by grace are ye saved through faith; and that not of yourselves: it is the gift of God"** (Eph. 2:8). We also must take full possession of our inheritance through battle. This is a warfare we cannot win on our own, but cannot lose with God's help. We also are to be strong and of a good courage as we also have the same promise that our enemies will not be able to stand before us. Jesus Christ defeated our enemies and secured our victory. As God was with Jesus, He is also with those who are in Christ to help them walk in victory. He will never fail or forsake His people.

We Prepare Ourselves With the Word

> **Only be thou strong and very courageous, that thou mayest observe to do according to all the law, which Moses my servant commanded thee: turn not from it to the right hand or to the left, that thou mayest prosper whithersoever thou goest. This book of the law shall not depart out of thy mouth; but thou shalt meditate therein day and night, that thou mayest observe to do according to all that is written therein: for then thou shalt make thy way prosperous, and then thou shalt have good success. Be strong and of a good courage; be not afraid, neither be thou dismayed: for the LORD thy God is with thee whithersoever thou goest. Then Joshua commanded the officers of the people, saying, Pass through the host, and command the people, saying, Prepare you victuals; for within three days ye shall pass over this Jordan, to go in to**

possess the land, which the Lord your God giveth you to possess it (Joshua 1:7-11).

God did not command the nation of Israel to prepare to go to war by means of carnal weapons. Their victory was to be obtained by observing God's Word. It was by walking in God's Word that caused them to be prosperous and successful. God's Word is full of examples of this. Israel always conquered their enemies when they were observing and walking in obedience to God's Word. They almost always suffered defeat when they were not. It did not matter how big or small their army was at the time. Small numbers of Israelites conquered huge numbers of adversaries when they were in obedience. Their biggest and most powerful armies were defeated when they were not.

This is just as important for us today as it was for the nation of Israel. The Old Testament scriptures are actually written to instruct the church (Rom. 15:4, 1 Cor. 10:1-11). Unlike theirs, our warfare is not against flesh and blood, but against principalities, against powers, against the rulers of the darkness of this world, against spiritual wickedness in high places (Eph. 6:12). We fight our warfare by God's Word and prayer. We put on every piece of God's armor by means of His Word (Eph. 6:11-17). God's Word is the truth that we are to have girt about our loins (Jn. 17:17). It reveals the righteousness of God which is our breastplate (Rom. 1:17). Our shield of faith comes from hearing God's Word (Rom. 10:17). Our helmet of salvation comes from being born of God's Word (1 Pet. 1:23). Our defensive weapon is the sword of the spirit, which is the Word of God. Jesus received victory over every one of the devil's temptations by quoting God's Word (Matt. 4:1-11).

Our victories come in the same way. We must keep sin out of our lives by knowing and walking in obedience to God's Word. We prepare ourselves for battle each time we study, pray, or meditate upon God's Word. God's Word actually builds strength and courage in our lives as it gives us the knowledge and assurance that God is with us (2 Chr. 15:8, 32:7-8).

Take the Battle to the Enemy

Another important lesson that we see here is that we should take the battle to the enemy. Many Christians never really go against our enemy but just attempt to ward off his attacks against them. This causes many to grow tired and weary. We should not wait for him to attack us before we go to battle. We should be taking the battle to him each and every day. We do this by God's Word and prayer. Jesus told us that He has given us power to tread on serpents and scorpions, and over all the power of the enemy: and nothing shall by any means hurt us (Lk. 10:19). That means we are to go against the enemy. Our victories, by taking the battle to him, will keep him under our feet where he belongs and can do us no harm.

Scripture also teaches us that God strengthens the hearts of those who are of good courage (Ps. 27:13-14, 31:24). We just need to be ready and on the spiritual battlefield each day. The Apostle Paul prayed for the Ephesian church to be strengthened with might by God's Spirit in the inner man (Eph. 3:16). This is something that each of us should pray for each day. We also receive strength and courage from one another as we come together and fellowship. We are to encourage and lift one another up.

Christians are often thought of as being weak. Much of this is because many see God's people walk in fear of the enemy, and pull back from the warfare that we are called to. Too many of God's people do not walk in victory. There is a real lack of confidence in much of the body of Christ. God's people should hold their heads up high, be strong and courageous, and take the battle to the enemy. To be a Christian is not to be weak and defenseless, but just the opposite.

Chapter 25

FIGHTING FOR OUR DELIVERANCES

The book of Judges gives us some excellent insight into our warfare. It clearly reveals the reasons why we suffer defeat, and how we are to obtain deliverances from the sins and strongholds that keep us in bondage. This book can be compared to the life believers live after salvation.

The events of the book of Judges begin after the death of Joshua. It first reports on the tribes of Israel going to war with the Canaanites that still remained in each of their inheritances. None of the tribes completely drove them out as they were commanded to. The Canaanites therefore dwelt in the land with them, and they did serve their gods just as God said they would. Because the people of Israel transgressed God's covenant, which He had made with their fathers, He would no longer drive out the nations which were left in the land after the death of Joshua. Instead, He used them to prove Israel, whether they would keep His ways, or not (Joshua chapters 1 & 2). Joshua 3:1-4 then states:

> Now these are the nations which the LORD left, to prove Israel by them, even as many of Israel as had not known all the wars of Canaan; Only that the

generations of the children of Israel might know, to teach them war, at the least such as before knew nothing thereof; Namely, five lords of the Philistines, and all the Canaanites, and the Sidonians, and the Hivites that dwelt in mount Lebanon, from mount Baal-hermon unto the entering in of Hamath. And they were to prove Israel by them, to know whether they would hearken unto the commandments of the LORD, which he commanded their fathers by the hand of Moses.

So the nation of Israel dwelt among the people of those nations, intermarried with them against God's command (Deut. 7:1-5), and served their gods. As a result the nation of Israel entered into a continuous cycle of forsaking the Lord to serve the gods of the land, be conquered by their enemies, and be put into bondage.

The anger of the Lord would be hot against Israel each time they forsook Him to serve other gods, and He would sell them into the hands of their enemies, who would spoil them and put them into bondage. God would leave them in bondage until they would cry out to Him because of it. He would then rise up a Judge to deliver them out of the hands of their enemies. Their deliverance would come through warfare. The Judge would often gather an army out of Israel. This would bring an attack against them from their captors. They would receive deliverance by defeating those who had them in captivity.

How this Applies to the Church

This is a picture of what can and does take place in our lives after salvation. Each Judge is a type of Jesus Christ whom God has raised up to deliver us from sin, and all the power of our enemy that attempts to hold us in bondage. Our enemies can only bring us back into bondage through sin, which does not have dominion in the life of a born again believer (Rom. 6:14).

The inhabitants (the Canaanites) of the land of Canaan are a type of our flesh. God does not take us out of this flesh, or remove the sin from it, when we come to salvation. However, He does give us the power to overcome it through the Spirit. He leaves us in this sinful body of flesh to prove us, whether we will keep His commandments, or not. It is also for the purpose of teaching us war. We do not know all that God has in store for us in the future, but it is obvious that He wants each of us to be taught war. The spiritual warfare we go through is necessary for what God is doing in our lives. As we all know, just because we are saved does not mean that sin does not remain a major battle in our lives. Certain sins can even have strongholds in our lives, which must be pulled down. Sin is the main reason we suffer defeat. A believer can always give into temptation and fall into sin. When a believer falls into sin, our enemy will spoil him of his spiritual blessings, and take him captive in that sin.

A believer can enter into a continuous cycle where he falls into a sin over and over again. He will remain in that condition until he seriously cries out to God for deliverance. When God then moves to bring deliverance, the enemy will also bring an attack against him to hold him in bondage. This is when a believer really needs to understand what is taking place in his life because he will enter into a very strong warfare. So strong that it can appear that God is doing nothing at all. Many fall at this point time and time again. This is when a believer needs to go against the enemy and receive their deliverance through the power of God. We will receive our victories through warfare. A serious spiritual attack usually means that God is moving to bring forth deliverance, or a blessing.

A born again believer once said, 'I don't like to pray because it just makes things harder.' He felt this way because he would pray for victory over the sin in his life and then enter into a warfare he did not understand. When God would move to deliver him, the enemy would bring an attack to hold him in bondage. The attack would be so strong that he would fall time and time again. Once he understood what was taking place, he stood strong in the warfare and received the victory.

The Example of Israel in Bondage to Egypt

For a good example of this, consider the nation of Israel when they were in bondage to Egypt. As soon as God sent Moses (a type of Christ) to deliver them, Pharaoh (a type of Satan) tightened his hold on them. For a time their bondage became harder rather than easier. Although God was at work to deliver them, they could not see or understand what was taking place. Most desired to just go back to the way it was before Moses arrived. It was through a continued warfare that they were finally delivered (Ex. 5).

Chapter 26

THE LAND OF GIANTS

Giants are spoken of frequently throughout much of the Old Testament. There has always been much speculation on who they were, and where they came from. A thorough study of the Word does hold the answers. A correct understanding reveals a powerful teaching for us today as we learn the meaning of the giants of the Old Testament.

The first reference that the bible makes to the giants is in Genesis chapter six. This reference also answers the questions of who they were, and where they came from. Gen. 6:1-2&4 states:

> **And it came to pass, when men began to multiply on the face of the earth, and daughters were born unto them, That the sons of God saw the daughters of men that they were fair; and they took wives of all which they chose. There were giants in the earth in those days; and also after that, when the sons of God came in unto the daughters of men, and they bare children to them, the same became mighty men which were of old, men of renown.**

Some believe that the 'sons of God' refer to the godly line of Seth (Adam's 3rd son), and the 'daughters of men' refer to the ungodly line of

Cain. A study of God's Word reveals that this cannot be true for two reasons. First, Genesis 6:4 tells us there were giants in the earth in those days, speaking of the days before the flood of Noah; and also after that, speaking of the days after the flood. Every other reference to the giants is after the flood, which completely destroyed Cain's lineage. Second, when a godly person comes together with an ungodly person they do not produce abnormal children. If that would be the case, Israel would have been filled with giants as they intermarried with the Canaanites, and many other ungodly nations. The result of this union between the sons of God and the daughters of men produced the race of giants that were once on the earth.

We will find that the sons of God were in reference to angelic beings. It refers here to the fallen angels. The Old Testament uses the phase 'sons of God' only three more times. All three times are in the book of Job and are clearly in reference to angelic beings (Job 1:6, 2:1, 38:7). Job 38:7 states, **"When the morning stars sang together, and all the sons of God shouted for joy?"** This verse of scripture makes it very clear as it is in reference to when the foundations of the earth was laid, before man was even created (see 38:4-7).

Further proof is also found in 2 Peter 2:4, which states, **"For if God spared not the angels that sinned, but cast them down to hell, and delivered them into chains of darkness, to be reserved unto judgment."** We know that the angels that fell with Satan are not yet chained up in hell reserved unto judgment, but are loose upon the earth in opposition to God and His people (Eph. 6:11-12, Lk. 10:19). Hell was prepared for the devil and his angels (Matt. 25:41), but the devil and most of the angels that fell with him have never been there yet. The sin that caused these angels to be thrown into hell is what is spoken of in Genesis chapter six. Jude also mentions these angels, saying, **"And the angels that kept not their first estate, but left their own habitation, he hath reserved in everlasting chains under darkness unto the judgment of the great day" (Jude 6).** This speaks of them leaving the habitation or realm of angels, and appearing unto men to marry their women. The bible makes many references of angels appearing in the form of men, and resembled a man in every way.

What is the message to the Church?

The giants of the Old Testament are to teach the spiritual man (the church) about the battles we must fight. Eph. 6:12 states,

> **For we wrestle not against flesh and blood, but against principalities, against powers, against the rulers of the darkness of this world, against spiritual wickedness in high places.**

No one in the Old Testament was born of God's Spirit. Their covenant was in their flesh (Gen. 17:18). They did not have any power or authority over the angelic beings in the spiritual realm. Their battles were outward in the flesh. There is no way a man of flesh can defeat an angelic being. It can only be done through the power of God. That is what God was showing us with the giants. The giants produced by the fallen angels made an enemy for the nation of Israel they could not defeat under their own power. In essence, it was a spiritual enemy manifested and fought through the flesh. This is to teach us about our enemy, and how we are to overcome them.

When the nation of Israel came to the land of Canaan after being delivered from Egypt, they sent twelve men to spy out the land. Ten of these spies brought back an evil report of the land, saying:

> **The land, through which we have gone to search it, is a land that eateth up the inhabitants thereof; and all the people that we saw in it are men of great stature. And there we saw the giants, the sons of Anak, which come of the giants: and we were in our own sight as grasshoppers, and so we were in their sight** (Num. 13:32b-33).

This first generation did not enter into the land because of unbelief. They saw an enemy they could not defeat by their own power and did not consider the power of God.

Only two from that first generation entered into the land. They were Joshua and Caleb, which were also two of the twelve men sent to spy out the land. These were men of faith. They did not look to their natural ability, but kept their eyes upon the omnipotent God, and put no limits on what He was able to do. They were fully ready to enter and conquer a land that scripture declared to be, 'A Land of Giants' (Deut. 3:13).

The second generation went in, under the leadership of Joshua, and conquered the land through the power of God. Joshua wholly followed all that God commanded him (Josh. 11:15), and was therefore able to conquer all the land and defeat the giants (Josh. 11:21-22). The name translated as Joshua from the Hebrew is translated as Jesus from the Greek. Joshua is a type of the resurrected Christ, and under His (Jesus) leadership, we can conquer every battle that comes against us.

The giants are a type of Satan and the demonic forces that fight against us. Just as those of Israel, many Christians consider the demonic spirits that fight against us as being too big and strong for us to overcome. This is true from a natural perspective. Just like Israel, God has made our enemies greater and mightier than we are according to the flesh. They are giants. An angelic being cannot be defeated through the flesh, but cannot stand against the power of God possessed by each born again believer. We just need to believe and walk in obedience to God's Word.

King David and Goliath

King David gives us an excellent example of how we are to go against our giants. As Israel warred with the Philistines, a giant by the name of Goliath would continually challenge anyone from the army of Israel to come out and fight him. As this man was almost ten feet tall, and a man of war, no one in the army of Israel dared to go out against him.

When David heard the challenge, he said, **"For who is this uncircumcised Philistine, that he should defy the armies of the living God"** (1 Sam. 17: 26b). To be uncircumcised meant that he was not in covenant with God. He therefore stood no chance against God's covenant people. David understood that to fight against the army of the living God was to fight against God Himself. He went against Goliath, who is a type of Satan, armed with a sling and five stones. However, he told Goliath:

> **"Thou comest to me with a sword, and with a spear, and with a shield: but I come to thee in the name of the LORD of hosts, the God of the armies of Israel, whom thou hast defied"** (1 Sam. 17:45).

He fought in the name of the Lord, which caused Goliath to fight against God. He killed the Philistine and brought a great deliverance to Israel.

The greatest weapon of our warfare is the name of Jesus. God has given every born again believer power through His name. As He is King of Kings and reigns over all of God's creation, everything must bow down and submit to His name. Nothing can resist the power of His name as nothing can resist Him. To call upon His name is to call upon Him. Jesus promised His people, **"And whatsoever ye shall ask in my name, that will I do, that the Father may be glorified in the Son. If ye shall ask any thing in my name, I will do it"** (Jn. 14:13-14).

However, these are not the only giants that can be in our lives. Certain sins, drug addictions, alcoholism, sex, money, or any number of things can also be a giant we must contend with. A giant might also be a sickness, disease, or an infirmity in our bodies. A giant is anything in our lives that we see as being too big and powerful to overcome or be delivered from. We must be like David and see that none of these things can stand up against the power of God. God has equipped us to walk in victory.

Chapter 27

MORE ARE THEY THAT ARE WITH US THAN THEY THAT ARE AGAINST US

The bible speaks of God's people as a remnant compared to the population of the world. To put it simply, the people of the world greatly outnumber God's people. At times this can make the warfare that we are called to seem almost impossible. For example, when God promised Abraham the land of Canaan as his inheritance, the Canaanites then inhabited the land (Gen. 12:6). If Abraham had looked at the overwhelming opposition in the natural, it would have seemed impossible for him to receive that land.

The nation of Israel experienced this firsthand. After being delivered from Egypt, which seemed impossible in itself, they were to conquer the land of Canaan and take it as their inheritance. Upon arriving at the border Moses sent out twelve men to spy out the land. Upon their return after searching the land for forty days, ten of the twelve said:

> We came unto the land whither thou sentest us, and surely it floweth with milk and honey; and this is the fruit of it. Nevertheless the people be to strong that

> **dwell in the land, and the cities are walled, and very great: and moreover we saw the children of Anak there. We be not able to go up against the people; for they are stronger than we. The land, through which we have gone to search it, is a land that eateth up the inhabitants thereof; and all the people that we saw in it are men of great stature. And there we saw the giants, the sons of Anak, which come of the giants: and we were in our own sight as grasshoppers, and so we were in their sight** (Num. 13:27-28, 31-33).

That first generation did not enter into the land because of their unbelief in God's ability to deliver the inhabitants of the land into their hands. They saw an enemy larger, stronger, and more numerous than themselves. They came to the conclusion that it was impossible to defeat them in battle. They looked through their natural eyes and saw an enemy they could not defeat by their own power, and did not look to the power of their supernatural God, or believe His Word.

Later, when preparing the second generation to enter into the land, Moses told them:

> **When the LORD thy God shall bring thee into the land whither thou goest to possess it, and hath cast out many nations before thee, the Hittites, and the Girgashites, and the Amorites, and the Canaanites, and the Perizzites, and the Hivites, and the Jebusites, seven nations greater and mightier than thou** (Deut. 7:1).

Moses informed them that God was going to deliver into their hands seven nations that were greater and mightier than they were. They were not to look at the size, numbers, or strength of their opposition in the natural, but to rely on God to deliver them into their hands.

The Spiritual Realm Governs the Natural Realm

It is necessary for God's people to be able to look at things spiritually rather than naturally. We will find that the spiritual realm governs the natural realm. What takes place in the natural realm is a manifestation of what has already transpired in the spiritual. For example, an angel appeared unto Daniel to give him the answer to a prayer that he had begun to pray for three weeks earlier. Upon arriving, the angel said unto Daniel:

> **Fear not, Daniel: for from the first day that thou didst set thine heart to understand, and to chasten thyself before thy God, thy words were heard, and I am come for thy words. But the prince of the kingdom of Persia withstood me one and twenty days: but, lo, Michael, one of the chief princes, came to help me; and I remained there with the kings of Persia** (Dan. 10:12-13).

The Persian Empire controlled the world at that time. The prince of the kingdom of Persia that withstood this angel (who was probably Gabriel) was the demon principality over the Persian Empire (Eph. 6:12). Michael, called one of the chief princes (that came to help him) is spoken of as an archangel, which stands up for the children of Israel (Dan. 12:1, Jude 9, Rev. 12:7). Upon departing from Daniel the angel was to return to fight with the prince of Persia. This was to bring forth the prince of Grecia. Greece later conquered Persia and was the next empire to come into power. God's angels had to defeat the principality over Persia for that empire to fall. This gave way for the prince (principality) over Greece to come forth (Dan. 10:20-21). Greece rose up and defeated Persia as a result of what had already taken place in the spiritual realm.

Jacob Saw into the Spiritual Realm

God's Word gives us several glances into this spiritual realm to reveal to us the spiritual forces that fight for God's people. The book of Genesis records the well-known story of Jacob and Esau, the twin brothers of Isaac. After Jacob tricked Isaac into giving him the blessing instead of his elder brother Esau, he then fled from Esau who hated him and had plans to kill him (Genesis chapter 27).

Twenty years later God told Jacob to return to the land of his fathers. Genesis 32:1-2 states, **"And Jacob went on his way, and the angels of God met him. And when Jacob saw them, he said, This is God's host: and he called the name of that place Mahanaim."** The name Mahanaim means two armies. This was in reference to the visible army consisting of Jacob and his servants, and the invisible army of God's angels. This was God revealing to Jacob that he was not alone. God's forces were there with him. Concerning these angels, Psalms 103:19-20 states:

> **Bless the LORD, ye his angels, that excel in strength, that do his commandments, hearkening unto the voice of his word. Bless ye the LORD, all ye his hosts, ye ministers of his, that do his pleasure.**

We learn from the New Testament that God's angels are ministering spirits sent forth to minister for them who shall be heirs of salvation (Heb. 1:14). A large part of their ministering is to fight for the safety and well being of God's children.

Jacob then sent servants before him to Esau. These servants returned saying that Esau was coming to Jacob with four hundred men. That could have only meant that Esau was planning to make his threat good. Jacob spent that night wrestling with God. When the two brothers finally met again the following day, they embraced one another. Jacob won the battle in the spirit before the two ever met in the natural.

King David Experienced the Spiritual Realm

When King David was at war with the Philistines, God told him:

> **Thou shalt not go up; but fetch a compass behind them, and come upon them over against the mulberry trees. And let it be, when thou hearest the sound of a going in the tops of the mulberry trees, that then thou shalt bestir thyself: for then shall the LORD go out before thee, to smite the host of the Philistines. And David did so, as the LORD had commanded him; and smote the Philistines from Geba until thou come to Gazar** (2 Sam. 5:23-25).

David defeated the Philistines because God's army had gone before him to defeat the opposition and secure the battle.

Elisha Saw into the Spiritual Realm

God's Word gives us another look into this spiritual realm during the time that Elisha was a prophet in Israel. At that time Syria warred against Israel. God would reveal unto Elisha the battle plans of the Syrian king, who would then inform the king of Israel. The king of Syria soon began to think that he had a spy among his servants. Then one of his servants told him about Elisha the prophet, who could tell the king of Israel the words the Syrian king spoke in his bedchamber (2 Ki. 6:8-14). After finding out that Elisha was in a city called Dothan, the Syrian army surrounded that city by night. The servant of Elisha rose up early in the morning only to discover that the city was surrounded with horses and chariots. He then asked Elisha:

> **Alas, my master! how shall we do?** Elisha responded, **Fear not: for they that be with us are more than they that be against us. Then Elisha prayed, and said, LORD, I pray thee, open his eyes, that he may see.**

> **And the LORD opened the eyes of the young man; and he saw: and, behold, the mountain was full of horses and chariots of fire round about Elisha** (2 Ki. 6:15-17).

Elisha then prayed for God to smite the Syrian army with blindness, which He did. Elisha then led the Syrian army into Samaria, which was the capital city of Israel. Once there, Elisha prayed for God to open their eyes. They then realized that they were in Samaria and had been taken captive by Israel. Once again, everything that took place in the natural realm was a result of what was taking place in the spiritual realm.

Jesus Christ Taught on the Spiritual Realm

Consider also the crucifixion of Jesus Christ. When the soldiers came to take Jesus the night before He was crucified, Peter drew a sword and cut off an ear to the servant of the high priest.

> **Then Jesus said unto him, Put up again thy sword into his place: for all they that take the sword shall perish with the sword. Thinkest thou that I cannot now pray to my Father, and he shall presently give me more than twelve legions of angels? But how then shall the scriptures be fulfilled, that thus it must be?** (Matt. 26:50-54).

These angels were available to Jesus had He needed and prayed for them. As heirs of salvation, the same thing holds true for us. God's angels are available to minister to us just as they were for Jesus. We just need to learn to utilize all that God has made available to us.

One legion was six thousand angels, which would have been far more than what would have been needed. Scripture often speaks of just one angel doing incredible things. The angel of the Lord, who is identified with the Lord Himself, killed 185,000 Assyrians in one night (2 Ki. 19:35). Psalms 34:7 says:

> **The angel of the LORD encampeth round about them that fear him, and delivereth them.**" Scripture also states, "**Ye are of God, little children, and have overcome them: because greater is he that is in you, than he that is in the world** (1 Jn. 4:4).

No matter what it looks like in the flesh, or with our natural eyes, the words of Elisha will always hold true. "**They that be with us are more than they that be against us.**" There is no need for us to ever turn away from the spiritual warfare we are called to because the opposition is too great. We just need to pray for God to open our eyes that we may see.

Chapter 28

TO THE VICTOR BELONGS THE SPOIL

God's Word makes it very clear that each and every born again believer is called into spiritual warfare. This is evident as we are chosen (in a sense drafted) to be soldiers of Jesus Christ (2 Tim. 2:3-4); with the main duty of a soldier to fight in a war. As our warfare is spiritual, it is not against flesh and blood: but against principalities, powers, rulers of the darkness of this world, and spiritual wickedness in high places (Eph. 6:12). Few believers really recognize the seriousness of this warfare or actively take a part in it. As a result, many easily suffer defeat and become the spoil of our enemy. Many remain held in bondage, serve the world rather (or more) than God's kingdom, live far below their benefits in Christ, and suffer the loss of many blessings.

God's people have always been called to warfare in both the Old and New Covenants. The nation of Israel was commanded to go to war with the Amalekites (Ex. 17:8-16, 1 Sam. 15:1-9), the Midianites (Num. 25:16-18, 31: 1-12), the Canaanites (Num. 33:52-53, Joshua chapters 6-12), and had to constantly defend themselves from attacks from the other nations. Although the nation of Israel did fight against flesh and blood, their warfare shows us examples and types designed to teach the church spiritual principles (1 Cor. 10:6-12). Their warfare was against flesh and blood because, under the Old Covenant, they had no power over the spiritual forces that war against God's people. Therefore, in order to stop the spiritual attack that was coming against them, they had to fight against the men that were being used as the instruments of the spiritual attacks.

The Taking of Spoil

The taking of spoil is almost always a part of war. This is clearly seen throughout the Old Testament scriptures which continually make reference to the victor of each battle gathering the spoil of their enemies. The nation of Israel was in no way excluded from this. God's Word clearly instructed them to also gather the spoil of their enemies. They were to get wealth and eat of the spoil of their enemies.

Many nations would go to war for the express purpose of taking the spoil of other nations. This would include bringing the nation conquered into servitude. When a walled city was conquered, the walls would be broken down leaving the people defenseless and servants to their conquerors.

Whenever Israel would suffer defeat, the walls of their fenced cities would be broken down, and anything of value was taken as spoil. They would also become servants to their captors. When the capital city of Jerusalem would suffer defeat, the treasures from the temple and from the king's house would be the first to be taken as spoil. This was because of the abundance of gold, silver, precious jewels, and other valuable items that would be found there (see 2 Chr. 12:1-9). Eventually, because of their sin, the temple was completely destroyed, and everything of value was carried away as spoil.

It is very important to understand that God's people suffer defeat as a result of sin (Josh. 7:11-12). Israel is a great example of this. Whenever we are not living in victory as children of God, it will usually always be as a result of sin in our lives. Those who keep sin out of their lives live confident, powerful, victorious Christian lives.

How This Applies to the Church

Let's look at the spiritual principles behind this, and see how it applies to those of the New Testament church. Our spiritual enemies come to spoil God's kingdom; especially His temple which is often spoken of as His house. The members of the body of Christ are the treasures of the King's house as each member is not only a stone in God's temple (1 Pet. 2: 5), but individual temples of God. 1 Cor. 3:16-17 states:

> **Know ye not that ye are the temple of God, and that the Spirit of God dwelleth in you? If any man defile the temple of God, him shall God destroy; for the temple of God is holy, which temple ye are.** 1 Cor. 6:19 **also states, What? know ye not that your body is the temple of the Holy Ghost which is in you, which ye have of God, and ye are not your own?**

The book of Hebrews also declares us to be God's house (Heb. 3:6).

We are the temples that the enemy comes to spoil and seeks to destroy. Scripture often compares God's Word to gold, silver, and precious jewels because of its value; especially in hearts of His people (Ps. 12:6, 19:10, Pro. 8:8-11). The gold, silver, and precious jewels found in the king's house and God's temple are therefore a type of God's Word, which is of the spoil the enemy comes to take. The enemy comes to spoil our bodies (God's temple) by taking or making us doubt God's Word, and tear down our walls of faith. He comes to bring us into bondage to do his service, along with those of our families. He comes to take our health, prosperity, and every other blessing that we have received from God. He comes to steal, kill and destroy (Jn. 10:10).

In the parable of the sower, the first attack of the enemy is to take away the Word that was sown in the hearts of those who heard it. Other attacks to take the Word come through tribulations and persecutions, or through the care and riches of the world (Mk. 4:1-9, 13-20). God's Word makes it clear that we are not to pollute God's house, which house we are, with the pollutions of the world. Otherwise, as the temple in Jerusalem, our temples can also be destroyed (2 Chr. 36:14-19, 1 Cor. 3:16-17).

As the taking of spoil is a part of war, God's people are not excluded. Once again, Israel is our example of this. The nation of Israel took the spoil of their enemies in accordance to God's Word. Deut. 20:10-14 states:

> **When thou comest nigh unto a city to fight against it, then proclaim peace unto it. And it shall be, if it make thee answer of peace, and open unto thee, then it shall be, that all the people that is found therein shall be tributaries unto thee, and they shall serve thee. And if it will make no peace with thee, but will make war against thee, then thou shalt besiege it: And when the LORD thy God hath delivered it into thine hands, thou shalt smite every male thereof with the edge of the sword: But the women, and the little ones, and the cattle, and all that is in the city, even all the spoil thereof, shalt thou take unto thyself; and thou shalt eat the spoil of thine enemies, which the LORD thy God hath given thee.**

Notice all that was taken as spoil. It was not limited to riches and livestock, but also included human captives.

Actually, all of God's people are taken as spoil from the world of whom Satan is the god of (2 Cor. 4: 4). The nation of Israel was delivered from Egypt, which, in scripture, is a type of the world. Upon their deliverance they even spoiled the nation of Egypt taking jewels of silver, gold, and raiment (Ex. 3:19-22, 12:35-36). This is significant as the tabernacle, which was built in the wilderness, and pointed to Christ and the church, was made of the very items taken from Egypt upon their deliverance.

The Spoil Profits All

Numbers chapter 31 records the account of Israel going to war against Midian at the command of God. This was because Midian had beguiled Israel to serve their gods. Israel was victorious and took an abundance of spoil, which included much livestock and virgin woman. All others were killed because they had beguiled Israel to serve their gods through the counsel of Balaam. The spoil was then divided to profit everyone in the nation. It was divided into two portions, with the greater portion divided between those who actually fought the war, and the lesser portion divided between those of the congregation.

At a later time in Israel's history, when David and his men were (supposedly) going to war with the Philistines, the Amalekites invaded the city of Ziklag where the families of David and his men were dwelling at that time. The Amalekites spoiled the city and took their wives, sons, and daughters as captives. After inquiring of God, who assured them that they would overtake them and recover all, David and his six-hundred men pursued after them. Along the way, two hundred became so faint that they could not continue the pursuit, and stayed behind with the stuff. The rest overtook them. In the battle that followed, according to God's promise, David and his men defeated the Amalekites and recovered all that they had lost, plus much more. When it was time to divide the spoil, some who fought the battle did not want to share the spoil with those who became weak and stayed behind. David then made it a statute and ordinance in Israel that the spoil was to be divided into two equal parts. One part was to go to those who fought the battle, and the other part to those who did not. David also sent of the spoil unto the elders throughout the cities of Judah, saying, "**Behold a present for you of the spoil of the enemies of the LORD**" (1 Sam. 30:1-31).

So, what does this all mean to the church, and how is it to be applied to our lives? Throughout our lives we fight many spiritual battles. Some we win, and others we lose. When we do suffer defeat it greatly affects us spiritually and naturally. The enemy takes the Word out of our hearts, weakens our faith, brings us into condemnation, and holds us in bondage to the world or certain sins that have strongholds in our lives. When this takes place to the leaders of any family or church, it can bring the entire family or congregation into bondage, and servants to the world. This does affect every area of our lives.

However, for every victory there are spoils that we can gather from our enemy that will profit all in the body of Christ. Strongholds can be broken and deliverance brought forth in our lives. Those taken captive by the devil can be retrieved and brought back into a right relationship with God. The world we once served can be made to serve us. Those who have become weak in the warfare can receive rest and strength. This may include financial breakthroughs, health, and the salvation of others. As people are taken as the spoils of war, the spoil of our victories may include the salvation of unsaved loved ones, or others that our lives may impact.

There is yet much spoil to be taken out of the world and brought into God's kingdom. Jesus stated, "**No man can enter into a strong man's house, and spoil his goods, except he first bind the strong man; and then he will spoil his house**." This was in reference to Satan who Jesus bound by defeating him in His death on the cross. We are to walk in the victory of Christ and spoil the kingdom of darkness.

Chapter 29

TAKING AWAY THE HIGH PLACES

A high place was a mountain, hilltop, or elevated site dedicated to the worship of pagan gods, which were most likely Canaanite in origin. A high place could consist of a sanctuary, shrine, altar and image.

At first, God commanded those of Israel to bring their sacrifices unto the door of the tabernacle of Moses, unto the priest, and offer them there unto the Lord. This was to prevent them from offering their sacrifices unto devils, after which they had previously gone a whoring (Lev. 17:1-7).

God also commanded Israel to utterly destroy all the places where the nations before them worshipped their gods. They were to offer their sacrifices and worship God in the place where He chose to put His name (Deut. 12:1-7). At first the tabernacle of Moses was placed in Shiloh, of the tribe of Ephraim, shortly after they entered into the land of their inheritance. However, Jerusalem was the place where God chose to put His name, and His temple was eventually built there.

Nevertheless, during the early period of Israel's history they did worship God in many of the high places that were in the land. This took place during the time of the Judges and into the reign of King Solomon, who built God's temple in Jerusalem. Once the temple was built, the prophets began to condemn the high places and command them to be taken away.

Israel Failed to Take Away the High Places

Many of the godly kings that reigned over Judah took necessary steps to remove idolatry from the nation, but fell short in taking away the high places. Scripture states concerning king Asa:

> **And Asa did that which was good and right in the eyes of the LORD, as did David his father. And he took away the sodomites out of the land, and removed the idols that his father had made. And also Maachah his mother, even her he removed from being queen, because she had made an idol in a grove: and Asa destroyed her idol, and burnt it by the brook Kidron. But the high places were not removed: nevertheless Asa's heart was perfect with the LORD all his days** (1 Ki. 15:11-14).

Many other kings such as Jehoshaphat, Jehoash, Amaziah, Azariah (Uzziah), and Jotham all did that which was right in the eyes of the Lord. However, concerning each of these kings, scripture also makes it a point to state, "**But the high places were not taken away: the people still sacrificed and burnt incense in the high places**" (1 Ki. 22:41-43, 2 Ki. 12:1-3, 14:1-4, 15:14, 32-35).

Many of these kings would tear down and destroy the altars and images, but the high place would not be taken away. These high places always left a foothold for idolatry to remain in Israel, and for the mixing of idolatry with the true worship of God.

How the High Places Apply to the Church

So how does this apply to us today? Each of us can also have high places in our lives where we secretly, or not so secretly, hold on to some idolatry. We do not need to bow down to an image of something to have idolatry in our lives. Anything that comes between God and us is an idol, and can cause a high place in our lives. We can worship material things such as houses, lands, cars, or money. We can also worship others, sex, pornography, a job, fame, ourselves, or even things we have accomplished. Philosophies of men such as humanism or naturalism are also types of idolatry that many have the tendency to mix with true Christianity. The love of this world and the things of this world are also high places where we syncretize the world into the true worship of God.

The taking away of our high places comes through the renewing of our minds. After all, our mind is our highest place. Just removing from our lives what we find to be idolatry might not be enough. We must also remove the thoughts of those things, or it leaves a foothold for them to remain in our lives. 2 Cor. 10:3-5 states:

> **For though we walk in the flesh, we do not war after the flesh: (For the weapons of our warfare are not carnal, but mighty through God to the pulling down of strongholds;) Casting down imaginations, and every high thing that exalteth itself against the knowledge of God, and bringing into captivity every thought to the obedience of Christ.**

Imaginations have to do with the ungodly 'images' we have put into our minds that continue to capture our thoughts. The high things are anything that exalts (lift up) itself against the knowledge of God. We will find idolatry wherever our thoughts are not brought into captivity to the obedience of Christ. We might have put them into our minds by viewing pornography, watching movies, playing video games, or other things we have done. All these things can become strongholds that must be pulled down by God's Word, prayer and fasting. Israel always remained subject to fall because the high places were never removed. It is a type of their mind never being renewed. The same thing holds true with us. Those who do not renew their minds through God's Spirit, and the study of His Word, will continually fall into sin.

God's Word reveals a number of things that are necessary for us to do to aid us in the renewing of our minds. We are to present our bodies as living sacrifices to God as a form of worship, and no longer be conformed (fashioned the same, same pattern) to this world. We can then be transformed by the renewing of our minds (Rom. 12:1-2). To continue in the same fashion and pattern of the world will keep this transformation (change) from taking place.

Along these same lines, Eph. 4:22-24 states:

> **That ye put off concerning the former conversation the old man, which is corrupt according to the deceitful lusts; And be renewed in the spirit of your mind, And that ye put on the new man, which after God is created in righteousness and true holiness.**

We are therefore to put away lying, anger, stealing, corrupt communication, bitterness, wrath, clamour, evil speaking and malice (Eph. 4:25-31). We are also to seek and set our affections on those things which are above, not on the things that are on the earth (see Col.3:1-10). Each of us can experience great godly change in our lives by taking away our high places.

Chapter 30

OBEDIENCE IS BETTER THAN SACRIFICE

God's Word clearly teaches that a lifestyle of obedience is far better than any sacrifice we can possibly make. Even when the nation of Judah was on the brink of destruction because of their disobedience, God did not instruct them to bring sacrifices, but to just turn (repent) from their sin and obey His voice. He let them know, through the prophet Jeremiah, that it was always about their obedience, not their sacrifices and offerings. Jeremiah 7:21-23 states:

> **For I spake not unto your fathers nor commanded them in the day that I brought them out of the land of Egypt, concerning burnt offerings or sacrifices: But this thing commanded I them, saying, Obey my voice, and I will be your God, and ye shall be my people: and walk ye in all that I have commanded you, that it may be well with you.**

The book of Jeremiah is a part of God's Word that each of us need to study thoroughly. Jeremiah was a last of the last day's prophet to the nation of Judah before they were conquered and scattered throughout the nations of the earth. The nation of Judah had drifted so far away from God, and obedience to His Word, that God's judgment was upon them; yet they could not see it. God continually instructed them to turn from their sin or His wrath would come upon them. As a result Jerusalem would be conquered, God's temple would be destroyed, and they that survived would be scattered throughout the nations of the earth. However, the people preferred to believe the false prophets who spoke of peace, and declared that God's wrath would not come upon Jerusalem, nor would He allow His temple to be destroyed; all of which came upon them.

Jeremiah chapter seven begins with God instructing Jeremiah to go and stand in the gate of the Lord's house, and speak to those who went in to worship Him. His message was for them to amend their ways, and not trust in the lying words of the false prophets (who spoke of peace), and God would not remove them from their land (Jer. 7:1-8). Verses 9-10 then state:

> **Will ye steal, murder, and commit adultery, and swear falsely, and burn incense unto Baal, and walk after other gods whom ye know not; And come and stand before me in this house, which is called by my name, and say, We are delivered to do all these abominations.**

Look at the activities of the people who went into the Lord's house to worship Him. These actually thought that because they worshipped in the Lord's house they could get away with doing these abominable acts. God does not deliver His people so that they can continue to live in sin.

The New Testament Church is No Different

In these last days of the New Testament church many have also drifted away from an obedient walk with God. Much of our view of God is limited to His love, and few preach on His anger or wrath anymore. There are more and more preachers who just speak on what the people want to hear. Much of the church tolerates all kinds of sexual immorality.

This even includes homosexually, which the bible declares to be an abomination to God. We have loved the world and refused to live as a holy (separated) sanctified people. It is often hard to tell the people of the church apart from the people of the world. Like Judah, much of our perspective of God has been clouded because of our carnality, and we have actually made ourselves comfortable living in disobedience. The people of the nation of Judah had never stopped bringing sacrifices to the temple, but they had stopped walking in obedience to God's Word. They believed that their sacrifices and offerings were sufficient to keep them in an acceptable position, and in right standing with God. Do not misunderstand, Christians are to live sacrificial lifestyles, but nothing can take the place or be more pleasing to God than a daily walk of obedience. Many Christians live carnal lifestyles and think that they can make up for it by a day of fasting, or by making an offering to the church, or by doing some kind of Christian service. God's Word clearly reveals that if we are not striving to obey His Word, these sacrifices are not pleasing to Him.

The Example of King Saul

The scriptures give us a perfect example of this with Saul, the first king that reigned over Israel. Under the threat of war from the Philistines, Saul offered burnt offerings and peace offerings to the Lord. This was in disobedience to God's Word as only a priest was able to make such offerings (see 1 Sam. 13:1-14). Saul felt that it was necessary for him to make these offerings, as he was not confident that God would be with him in the war; and Samuel, who was a priest, was nowhere to be found. This lack of confidence could only have been a result of a questionable lifestyle before God. Believers that walk in constant obedience to God's Word have the confidence to know that God will be there for them in any circumstance. They do not have to get in their prayer closets, confess sins, and try to make peace with God during times of trouble. As a result of this act of disobedience, God would not establish Saul's kingdom to continue after him. There is a consequence to our every act of disobeying God's Word.

At a later time, God commanded King Saul to go to war with Amalek and utterly destroy all that they had. He was to spare no one, or leave anything alive. However, Saul spared the king of Amalek and the best of the livestock. When confronted by Samuel the prophet concerning his disobedience, Saul insisted that he had kept the commandment of the Lord as he had destroyed all that was vile and refuse, but had kept the best of the sheep and oxen to sacrifice to the Lord. Samuel responded by saying:

> **Behold, to obey is better than sacrifice, and to hearken than the fat of rams. For rebellion is as the sin of witchcraft, and stubbornness is as iniquity and idolatry. Because thou hast rejected the word of the LORD, he hath also rejected thee from being king** (1 Sam. 15: 22b-23).

No amount of sacrifices can take the place or make up for deliberate acts of disobedience. To disobey is to reject God's Word, and sacrifice the position of authority that all believers have in Christ.

Notice also, Saul's partial obedience was not good enough, nor was he praised or given any credit for it. His disobedience negated the part of the Word, which he actually kept. At first, he insisted that he had kept the commandment of the Lord as he had performed almost all of it. The part he did not fully keep he claimed was for a good reason. After all, what could be more important than making sacrifices to God?

Many Christians are No Different

Many Christians live this kind of lifestyle. We obey in certain (maybe even most) areas of our lives, but not in all, and still believe that our lifestyle is acceptable with God. It is time to quit fooling ourselves, and strive to bring our lives in obedience to God's Word. Of course we are not going to live lives free from sin as long as we are living in these sinful bodies of flesh, but we are to strive to walk in obedience. There is never an excuse to deliberately disobey God's Word. A true salvation experience does bring a change in the way a person lives, as we do receive God's divine nature when we receive the Holy Spirit (2 Pet. 1:3). Sin does not have dominion in the lives of God's people (Rom. 6:14). Someone truly born again can never sin as they did before, and certain things are never to be a part of our lives after salvation. 1 Cor. 6:9-11 states:

> **Know ye not that the unrighteous shall not inherit the kingdom of God? Be not deceived: neither fornicators, nor idolaters, nor adulterers, nor effeminate, nor abusers of themselves with mankind, Nor thieves, nor covetous, nor drunkards, nor revilers, nor extortioners, shall inherit the kingdom of God. And such were some of you: but ye are washed, but ye are sanctified, but ye are justified in the name of the Lord Jesus, and by the Spirit of the living God.**

Simply put, Christians have no excuse to commit the sins that God saved and freed us from. They are not to be a part of our lives. Eph. 5:4-7 also states:

> **But fornication, and all uncleanness, or covetousness, let it not be once named among you, as becometh saints; Neither filthiness, nor foolish talking, nor jesting, Which are not convenient: but rather giving of thanks. For this we know, that no whoremonger, nor unclean person, nor covetous man, who is an idolater, hath any inheritance in the kingdom of Christ and of God. Let no man deceive you with vain words: for because of these things cometh the wrath**

of God upon the children of disobedience. Be not ye therefore partakers with them.

Those who commit these sins need to examine themselves to see if they are even in the faith (2 Cor. 13:5), for God's Word clearly states that those who commit such acts will not inherit His kingdom.

Israel's Sacrifices Without Obedience

In the first chapter of Isaiah, God refers to Israel as Sodom and Gomorrah, asking them what the purpose was for the multitude of the sacrifices they offered Him. He called them vain oblations and abominations, along with their keeping of the new moons, and Sabbaths, and solemn meetings. Nothing they offered was accepted or received because it was not accompanied with an obedient lifestyle (Isa. 1:10-15).

We often make our walk with God harder than it needs to be. When we find our walk with God difficult, it is usually because of a lack of obedience on our part. God's Word states that the way of the transgressor is hard (Pro. 13:15). Actually, His commandments are not grievous (1 Jn. 5:3). God has made it very simple. Micah 6:6-8 states:

> **Wherewith shall I come before the LORD, and bow myself before the high God? Will the LORD be pleased with thousands of rams, or with ten thousands of rivers of oil? Shall I give my firstborn for my transgression, the fruit of my body for the sin of my soul? He hath showed thee, O man, what is good, and what doth the LORD require of thee, but to do justly, and to love mercy, and to walk humbly with thy God?** Hos. 6:6 also states, **For I have desired mercy, and not sacrifice; and the knowledge of God more than burnt offerings.**

Chapter 31

THE DANGER OF COMPROMISE

Each of us should desire a close, intimate, personal relationship with God. We should desire to be effectively used by God as we live out our lives upon this earth. Every compromise we make will limit these things from taking place in our lives. Some compromises are knowingly made, with many not seeming to be that big of a deal. We mistakenly do not believe that they will noticeably affect our spiritual lives. Other compromises we are tricked into making by the craftiness of our adversary. God's Word gives us clear warning signs and reveals the things we need to look out for.

As soon as God begins to move in a person's life, Satan tightens his grip in an attempt to keep that person from coming to salvation. Then after salvation, he remains at work by putting obstacles or circumstances in our lives in an attempt to get us to compromise.

To compromise is easy to do, even by those who have walked with God for many years. When Dinah, Jacob's daughter, compromised by going out to see the daughters of the land, she was taken by a prince of the Hivites and sexually defiled. Jacob then also seemed willing to compromise by intermarrying with the Hivites to avoid trouble with the people of the land. This was contrary to what he knew to be the will of God for Israel. God did not permit this to happen as Israel would have become one people with the Hivites, and no longer the chosen nation He had called them to be (see Genesis chapter 34).

Pharaoh Attempts to get Moses to Compromise

We have some excellent examples in the book of Exodus. It is commonly known and taught that Egypt is a type of the world system, and Pharaoh is a type of Satan. God delivering His people out of Egypt is a type of salvation, where we are delivered from the world, and the power of darkness (Satan).

As soon as Moses and Aaron gave God's message to Pharaoh instructing him to, "**Let my people go**", Pharaoh increased their workload and even removed the straw that was needed for them to make bricks (Exodus chapter 5). In much the same way, Satan will bring burdens from the world upon us to hold us in bondage and prevent us from serving the Lord. Just because God begins to move in a person's life does not mean that everything is going to go smoothly. Satan will always intervene in an attempt to keep us from receiving what God has for us.

As we all know, Pharaoh refused to let the Israelites go, so God began to bring a number of Plagues upon Egypt. As each plague would loosen the hold that Pharaoh had on God's people, he soon began to offer them compromises. After the fourth plague, which was swarms of flies, Pharaoh called for Moses and Aaron, and said, "**Go ye, sacrifice to your God in the land**" (Ex. 8:25). As Egypt is a type of the world, this compromise is designed to keep God's people living life in the world much like they did before. It implies that I can be a Christian and still continue to live a worldly life. Sadly to say, Satan does not have to bring any other compromise to many people. Many readily accept this compromise, and if they actually receive salvation, live very carnal lives. It is often hard to tell the people of the church apart from the people of the world. The real truth of the matter is that we cannot serve God and remain in the world. Moses responded to this compromise by saying:

> **It is not meet so to do; for we shall sacrifice the abomination of the Egyptians to the LORD our God: lo, shall we sacrifice the abomination of the Egyptians before their eyes, and will they not stone us?** (Ex. 8:26).

A true Christian lifestyle is an abomination to the people of the world. It requires that we make sacrifices and refuse to live our lives as the people of the world do. This brings persecution to our lives. 2 Tim. 3:12 states, **"Yea, and all that will live godly in Christ Jesus shall suffer persecution."** If we are not suffering persecution we are not living godly lives in Christ Jesus. Jesus warned us that the world would hate and persecute us (Jn. 15:18-20). If it does not, we have compromised.

Moses then said:

> **We will go three days journey into the wilderness, and sacrifice to the LORD our God, as he shall command us. Pharaoh then suggested, I will let you go, that ye may sacrifice to the LORD your God in the wilderness; only ye shall not go very far away: entreat for me** (Ex. 8:27-28).

Even though these terms seemed more agreeable to Moses, Pharaoh's agenda remained the same. This was actually another compromise. The closer we stay to the world the easier it is to bring us back again. This compromise implies that I can be a Christian and still keep close ties to the world. I do not have to separate myself from ungodly friends or take my Christian walk to any extremes. I can live my life as a Christian, and when I am away from the church, have quick access back to the world. These compromises have caused many to live the lukewarm life that we are warned about in God's Word (Rev. 3:15-16).

Pharaoh's next attempt to get Moses to compromise was to let the men go and serve the Lord, but leave their families in Egypt (Ex. 10:8-11). This compromise implies that I can be a Christian without being the spiritual head and priest over my household. It also implies that I can be married to a worldly person, and love that which is in the world (1 Jn. 2:15-17). If that which I love is in (of) the world, I will always go back to it. God's Word makes it very clear that if we marry an unsaved person, that person will turn our hearts away from serving the Lord (Deut. 7:3-4).

Pharaoh's last compromise to Moses was:

> **Go ye, serve the LORD; only let your flocks and your herds be stayed: let your little ones go also with you. And Moses said, Thou must give us also sacrifices and burnt-offerings, that we may sacrifice unto the LORD our God. Our cattle also shall go with us; there shall not an hoof be left behind; for thereof must we take to serve the LORD our God; and we know not with what we must serve the LORD, until we come thither.**

This compromise implies that I can be a Christian without living a sacrificial lifestyle. God's Word instructs us to present our bodies as living sacrifices, holy, acceptable unto God, which is our reasonable service (Rom. 12:1). We serve God by being a living (not dead as the OT sacrifices) sacrifice and living a sacrificial lifestyle. If Israel had accepted any of these compromises, they would not have been completely delivered from Egypt.

Compromise Let's the Enemy In

Let's look at another example in the book of Ezra. The events in Ezra took place shortly after the seventy-year Babylonian captivity. The Persian King, Cyrus, permitted many of the Jewish people to return to

Jerusalem to rebuild God's temple. The land of Israel was then inhabited by people of many different nations that had been placed there by the king of Assyria, who had conquered those nations before the rise of the Babylonian Empire (2 Ki. 17:24-41, Ezra 4:2).

Once the work was started and the foundation of the temple was laid (Ezra 3:8-13), their adversaries (people of the other nations used by Satan) quickly showed up on the scene. Ezra 4:1-4 states:

> **And when the adversaries of Judah and Benjamin heard that the children of the captivity builded the temple unto the LORD God of Israel; They came to Zerubbabel, and to the chief of the fathers, and said unto them, Let us build with you: for we seek your God, as ye do; and we do sacrifice unto him since the days of Esarhaddon king of Assur, which brought us up hither. But Zerubbabel, and Jeshua, and the rest of the chief of the fathers of Israel, said unto them, Ye have nothing to do with us to build an house unto our God; but we ourselves together will build unto the LORD God of Israel, as king Cyrus the king of Persia hath commanded us.**

Remember, the building of the temple is a type of Jesus Christ building the church, which is spoken of as God's house or temple throughout the New Testament.

The adversaries of Judah and Benjamin came to them under a cloche of friendship and fellow worshippers of the God of Israel. This was an attempt to get them to compromise.

Satan does not appear with a red tail and horns like many of us picture him, but is transformed into an angel of light. His ministers can also therefore appear as the ministers of righteousness (2 Cor. 11:14-15).

This could have outwardly appeared to be a good opportunity. It could have even been mistaken to be a move from God sending them help to do the work He had sent them to do. To accept this compromise would have welcomed the enemy into their midst. An enemy on the inside can do far more damage than one that is without. He can cause division, envy, strife and confusion. This can divide the true members (builders) and make the temple weak and unstable. As these adversaries worshipped many different gods, they would have subtly introduced their doctrines and the worship of their gods into the temple worship of the God of Israel.

This is exactly what has taken place in the church today. We welcome almost anyone that claims to be a Christian regardless of the life they live or the fruit they bear. We have welcomed our adversaries to build with us, and they have scattered the flock by false doctrines and traditions of men. This is clearly seen by all the different teachings and doctrines on the same subject matters. This has divided the church into countless denominations.

By giving in to so many of these compromises much of the church has lost sight of what it is to be a true Christian. Many confessing Christians have no idea what it really is to be born of God's Spirit. Christianity has been so deluded by the world that it is widely thought of as just another religion, with nothing really special about it. We need to recognize where we have made compromises, no matter how small, and begin to filter the world out of the church.

Chapter 32

THE RESULTS OF SIN IN A BELIEVERS LIFE

And the LORD God commanded the man, saying, Of every tree of the garden thou mayest freely eat: But of the tree of the knowledge of good and evil, thou shalt not eat of it: for in the day that thou eatest thereof thou shalt surely die (Gen. 2:16-17).

We know from scripture that sin entered into the world as a result of Adam's disobedience to the command of God not to eat of the tree of the knowledge of good and evil. The first result of sin was death. God informed Adam that in the day he ate of the tree of the knowledge of good and evil he would die. We know that Adam did eat of the tree he was commanded not to, but then lived for hundreds of years afterward. So, Did Adam die in the day he ate of the tree, or not? The answer is yes. Adam died spiritually in the day he ate of the forbidden tree. Spiritual death is to be separated from God, the only true source of life. The natural death followed later as a result of the spiritual death. **"Wherefore, as by one man sin entered into the world, and death by sin; and so death passed upon all men, for that all have sinned"** (Rom. 5:12).

No One is Without Sin

Each and every person on earth is a descendant of Adam. When he sinned he took all mankind with him. We were all in his loins and were just as much corrupted by sin as Adam himself. King David stated, **"Behold, I was shapen in iniquity; and in sin did my mother conceive me"** (Ps. 51:5). Scripture also states that before a person is saved (quickened, given life) they are dead (separated from God) in trespasses and sins.

True believers have redemption and forgiveness from sin through the blood of Jesus Christ (Eph. 1:7, Col. 1:14). The spiritual birth (born again) places each believer IN CHRIST. The law of the spirit of life in Christ Jesus makes us free from the law of sin and death (Rom. 8:2). 1 Cor. 15:21-22 states,

> **For since by man came death, by man came also the resurrection of the dead. For as in Adam all die, even so in Christ shall all be made alive.**

Nevertheless, even though born again believers are free from the law of sin and death, this does not mean that we have no sin. 1 Jn. 1:8 states, **"If we say that we have no sin, we deceive ourselves, and the truth is not in us"**. As long as we remain in this sinful body of flesh there will always be the presence of sin, which will eventually result in the death of the natural body. However, we are no longer slaves to sin, nor does it any longer have dominion over us (Jn. 8:34, Rom. 6:14). God's Word instructs believers not to give into the temptations that will bring forth sin in our lives, and to confess the sins we do commit for forgiveness and cleansing (1 Jn. 1:9).

Believers are therefore in no way impervious to sin. James 1:14-15 tells us:

> **But every man is tempted, when he is drawn away of his own lust, and enticed. Then when lust hath**

> conceived, it bringeth forth sin: and sin, when it is finished, bringeth forth death.

This is how sin entered into the world to begin with, and it is still how believers are overcome with sin today. Think about it. The serpent in the garden tempted Eve when she was drawn away of her own lusts, and enticed. She saw that the tree was good for food (the lust of the flesh), pleasant to the eyes (the lust of the eyes), and to be desired to make one wise (the pride of life; Gen. 3:6, 1 Jn. 2:15-17). When the lust had conceived it brought forth sin, which when finished brought forth death.

Believer's Should Strive to Overcome Sin

There are many believers who strive to overcome sin and keep it out of their lives, but there are also many who do not. Many seem to have the attitude that we are always going to sin, but God understands and it therefore does not really affect our lives or our relationship with Him. Nothing could be farther from the truth. Sin not only dramatically affects our individual lives and relationships with God, but it also affects the entire body of Christ.

> **Behold, the LORD'S hand is not shortened, that it cannot save; neither his ear heavy, that it cannot hear: But your iniquities have separated between you and your God, and your sins have hid his face from you** (Isa. 59:1-2).

The effects of sin are always the same. It works death in a person's life. Remember, spiritual death is to be separated from God. Iniquity separates us from God, and sin hides his face from us that He will not hear our prayers. Ps. 66:18 states, **"If I regard iniquity in my heart, the LORD will not hear me."** Our prayers often go unheard because of the sin we refuse to give up, or do not strive to get out of our lives. Confessing sins over and over again does not put a person back in a right relationship with God if that person plans to continue in that sin. For example, if I look on women to lust after them in my heart, my prayer of confession will not be heard if I plan on going to the beach tomorrow for the purpose of looking at women to lust after them.

Sin separates us from God and stops the power of God from working in our lives. Many of us do not experience God or the power of the Holy Ghost because we continue to live in sin. God's Word states in Jeremiah 5:25, **"Your iniquities have turned away these things, and your sins have withholden good things from you."** The things God was referring to in this verse was the former and latter rains in their season, and God reserving to Israel the appointed weeks of the harvest (Jer. 5:24). It is interesting to note that the former and latter rains are often referred to as a type of the outpouring of God's Spirit. It is our iniquities and sins that turn away the outpouring of God's Spirit upon us as individuals, and upon the church as a whole. God has an abundance of good things for us that have been turned away and withheld from us by our sins.

Sin affects the Entire Body of Christ

It is the responsibility of every child of God to learn and walk in obedience to God's Word. God's Word states, **"for by the law is the knowledge of sin"** (Rom. 3:20), and that **"sin is the transgression of the law"** (1 Jn. 3:4). Sin is never acceptable in the life of any believer. It not only affects the person who commits the sin, but the entirety of the body of Christ. 1 Corinthians 12:12-27 pictures the church as one man with each believer as a member of that one body. Each member is placed in the body and tempered together by God. This is done so that there is no division or separation in the body. Each member affects every other member of the body. If one member suffers, every other member suffers with it. For example, if any member (part) of a natural body is injured, it affects the operation of the entire body. If one member is honored, all rejoice with it. If one member is in sin, it brings the whole body into sin, as we are members one of another. Every action of each member affects the body as a whole.

The Effects of the Sin of Achan

God gave us a natural example of this with the nation of Israel, which is also often referred to as a single body, or one man (Isa. 1:5-6, Jud. 20:1, 8, 11). After delivering them from Egypt, God instructed them to put to death any person, or those of a city, that turned away from following Him by worshipping other gods, shedding innocent blood, bearing false witness, rebellion, or adultery (Deut. 13, 17:2-14, 19, 21:22-24). This was to be done for the purpose of putting away the evil from among them.

Israel realized the importance of this very soon after entering into their promised land. Their very first battle was against the walled city of Jericho. God declared the city to be accursed. They were to destroy every living thing in the city and consecrate all the silver, gold, brass, and iron unto the Lord. They were to take none of the spoil for themselves, or they themselves would become accursed like that which they took from the accursed city (Joshua 6, Deut. 7:26).

After defeating Jericho, they proceeded to what appeared to be the insignificant city of Ai, where they were defeated and fled before their enemies. When they inquired of the Lord as to why, God said:

> **Israel hath sinned, and they have also transgressed my covenant which I commanded them: for they have even taken of the accursed thing, and have also stolen, and dissembled also, and they have put it even among their own stuff. Therefore the children of Israel could not stand before their enemies, but turned their backs before their enemies, because they were accursed: neither will I be will you any more, except ye destroy the accursed from among you** (Joshua 7:11-12).

A man by the name of Achan had secretly taken of the spoils of Jericho and buried it under his tent. His sin was laid to the charge of all Israel, as he was a member of that nation (or body). The sin of this one man brought the whole nation into sin. As the sin separated them from God, it stopped the power of God in the nation, and they could not stand before their enemies. Once the sin was found out, Achan, along with all his family (who apparently knew) and livestock were stoned. They were then burned with fire along with all that he possessed. This was to show the complete removal of the sin from the nation.

This is just one of many examples in God's Word of God's people suffering defeat because of sin. Their sin would also often bring an attack of the enemy against them. Without God being with them they would be conquered and brought into bondage and made to serve their enemies.

Separation is the Only Solution

We have become far too tolerant of sin in the church today. We also need to put away the evil from among us by separating ourselves from those who refuse to live holy lifestyles. The New Testament does instruct us to do so. In Paul's first letter to the Corinthians, he instructed them to put away from among them a man who was committing fornication with his father's wife (1 Cor. 5:1-2). He instructed them **"to deliver such an one unto Satan for the destruction of the flesh, that the spirit may be saved in the day of the Lord Jesus"** (1 Cor. 5:5). He went on to inform them that a little leaven leavens the whole lump. The bible often uses leaven in reference to sin, as the effects are the same. In other words, this man's sin was affecting the whole church. It not only brought the entire church into sin, but if left unmoved, that sin would also spread throughout the congregation.

God's Word also gives us examples of this. Sodom, Gomorrah, and the other cities of the plains were all overtaken with the sin of homosexuality. God's people are in no way immune to sin if it's not dealt with in the church body. At one time, the tribe of Benjamin was almost completely destroyed as a result of this same sin. Once it got started, it spread throughout the tribe. The other tribes of Israel had to go to war against them to remove that sin from Israel (Judges 19-21).

1 Corinthians chapter five goes on to instruct the church not to keep company with any man that calls himself a brother, but is a fornicator, or covetous, or an idolater, or a railer, or a drunkard, or an extortioner. We are not even to eat with such a person. It is a common thing in the church today to encourage those living in sin to remain in the church. We have been under the false impression that they are better off in the church than to be removed. In so doing we permit them to continue in their sin, and we all pay a price for it. There are many sins that are absolutely forbidden by God's Word that are common in the church today. We have become the lukewarm church we read about in God's Word. The man who was removed from the Corinthian church repented as a result, and was then let back in the church (2 Cor. 2:6-8). It is an example that needs to be followed.

The bible is filled with other examples; but all we really need to do is look at the condition of the church. It is a rare thing to really see or experience the power of God that we read about in the bible. It can only be sin that turns away God's power and withholds good things from us. For all of us who really desire to experience the power of God in our lives, it is necessary for us to walk in obedience to God's Word and separate ourselves from all who do not.

Chapter 33

THE SIN OF PRIDE

"An high look, and a proud heart, and the plowing of the wicked, is sin" (Proverbs 21:4).

Pride is to lift up and exalt oneself. It is the attitude of being above or superior to others. Pride is to be inflated with self-conceit, high minded, boastful, pretentious, arrogant, despiteful, and even injurious to others. However, pride does not have to appear in an outward show, but can also be an inward attitude of the heart. It is in essence a form of self-worship.

The nature of pride is that of an independent and selfsufficient spirit that leads one to rebel against God. It causes a man to deny or forget that he is a created being, and exalt himself against God. It makes a person to ignore God and attempt to control his or hers own life and future. We are taught in scripture that pride is what lead Satan to rebel against God (Ezek. 28:17, 1 Tim. 3:6), was the iniquity of Sodom (Ezek. 16:49), and is blamed for man's insolent rejection of God's salvation. Psalms 10:4 states, **"The wicked, through the pride of his countenance, will not seek after God: God is not in all his thoughts."**

How God Feels About Pride

It is clear to see just how serious of a matter that pride really is. It is no wonder when scripture gives a list of the things that God hates, pride is at the very top of the list.

Proverbs 6:16-19 states:

> **These six things doth the LORD hate: seven are an abomination unto him: A proud look, a lying tongue, and hands that shed innocent blood, An heart that deviseth wicked imaginations, feet that be swift in running to mischief, A false witness that speaketh lies, and he that soweth discord among brethren.**

Concerning our fear (reference) of the Lord, Proverbs 8:13 states, "**The fear of the LORD is to hate evil: pride, and arrogancy, and the evil way, and the froward mouth, do I hate.**" Once again, pride is at the top of the list.

Each one of us has some degree of pride in our lives. It is a serious problem for many Christians as it keeps them from developing a close relationship with God. It is written, "**God resisteth the proud, but giveth grace unto the humble**" (James. 4:6, 1 Pet. 5:5). To resist means to come against, oppose, combat and withstand. As the nature of pride is to rebel against Him, God actually comes against and pushes away those who live in pride.

Pride Diminishes Our View of God

Psalms 138:6 also states, "**Though the LORD be high, yet hath he respect unto the lowly: but the proud he knoweth afar off.**" These scriptures are not speaking of the people of the world, but those of the church. As God knows the proud afar off, a prideful person can never draw close to Him or really come to know Him. It is much like a mountain range that is seen from a long distance. Even though its peaks rise thousands of feet high, they actually look small from far away; nor can any details of the mountains be seen. The rock formations, different colors, flowers, trees, and grass cannot be seen from a far distance. Only when one gets close to the mountains do their true sizes really appear. Only then can one see all the different details and beauty that cannot be seen from far away.

That is exactly what pride does to our view of God as a prideful person wants to be independent, self-sufficient and in control of his own life. God plays a small role in that person's life. Others see little evidence of God in a prideful person's life, and God appears much smaller to the prideful compared to what He really is. It is only through humility (the opposite of pride) that one can draw close to God, begin to see His size and power, and all His manifold, multifaceted attributes. Each of us needs to really understand what is being taught here, and carefully examines our lives because it applies to so many of us. We need to ask ourselves the questions: Does God seem close or far off? Does He appear bigger than any of my problems, or whatever I might be going through? How clearly do I really see and know His different attributes?

How the World Feels About Pride

The world actually considers pride to be a positive thing 1 John 2:15-17 tells us:

> **Love not the world, neither the things that are in the world. If any man love the world, the love of the Father is not in him. For all that is in the world, the lust of the flesh, the lust of the eyes, and the pride of life, is not of the Father, but is of the world. And the world passeth away, and the lust thereof: but he that doeth the will of God abideth forever.**

From a worldly perspective it is a positive thing to lift up, exalt, and think high of one self. People are often encouraged to put themselves first and go after what they want, even if it means trampling over others to get it. It is often said that we should think highly of ourselves, take pride in ourselves and in the things, which we do. Pride can be included in what Jesus was referring to when he said, **"Ye are they which justify yourselves before men; but God knoweth your hearts: for that which is highly esteemed among men is abomination in the sight of God"** (Lk. 16:15). After all, the Word does say that the proud in heart is an abomination to the Lord (Pro. 16:5).

Pride can therefore be very deceiving. Speaking of God's judgment upon Edom, Obadiah 3-4 states:

> **The pride of thine heart hath deceived thee, thou that dwellest in the clefts of the rock, whose habitation is high; that saith in his heart, Who shall bring me down to the ground? Though thou exalt thyself as the eagle, and though thou set thy nest among the stars, thence will I bring thee down, saith the Lord.**

Pride not only affected Edom, but it also had a dramatic effect upon Israel. Hosea 5:5 states, **"And the pride of Israel doth testify to his face: therefore shall Israel and Ephraim fall in their iniquity; Judah also shall fall with them."** Pride causes any person or nation to fall in their iniquity. No country (not even America) or person that lifts themselves up is safe from God's judgment and wrath. God's Word will always prove itself to be true. **"Pride goeth before destruction, and an haughty spirit before a fall"** (Pro. 16:18).

As we can clearly see, pride is a condition of the heart. It is one of a list of things that Jesus said comes forth from the heart (Mk. 7:22). Scripture also says that pride hardens our minds (Dan. 5:20). As the proud in heart is an abomination to the Lord, it brings God's wrath upon those who are guilty. As we can also see, God's people are in no way immune.

For example, Hezekiah, a godly king that reigned over Judah, found his heart lifted up with pride. 2 Chr. 32:24-26, states:

> **In those days Hezekiah was sick unto death, and prayed unto the LORD: and he spake unto him, and gave him a sign. But Hezekiah rendered not again according to the benefit done unto him; for his heart was lifted up: therefore there was wrath upon him, and upon Judah and Jerusalem. Notwithstanding Hezekiah humbled himself for the pride of his heart, both he and the inhabitants of Jerusalem, so that the wrath of the LORD came not upon them in the days of Hezekiah.**

The remedy for pride is to humble oneself before the Lord, and stay humble.

Chapter 34

A HUMBLE SPIRIT

"**Better it is to be of a humble spirit with the lowly, than to divide the spoil with the proud**" (Pro. 16:19).

Humility is a Christian characteristic developed in believers as we grow through the study of the Word, and the working of God's Spirit. It is the opposite of pride, which is a characteristic of the world. It is an attitude of lowliness in acknowledgement that all that one has, and is, comes from the Almighty God; the only true high and lofty One. It is to voluntarily submit oneself under His mighty hand. It is not to be or feel inferior or lower than other people, or to have an inferiority complex. It is to recognize one's state and standing with God, and to live one's life accordingly.

Many are under the false impression that to be humble is to be weak and to let others take advantage of them. Many also feel that humility will keep them from achieving what they feel they are capable of. You know it is a dog eat dog world. Actually the opposite is true. Proverbs 22:4 states, "**By humility and the fear of the LORD are riches, and honour, and life.**"

The bible says that God resists the proud, but gives grace unto the humble (James. 4:6, 1 Pet. 5:5). He therefore opposes those who walk in pride, but defends and helps those who walk in humility. The humble have God on their side. He will exalt the person who humbles himself or herself before God, in their humility. God's Word states, "**For whosoever exalteth himself shall be abased; and he that humbleth himself shall be exalted**" (Matt. 23: 12, Lk. 14: 11, 18: 14). The end result of pride is to be abased, and the end result of humility is to be exalted. The exact opposite of what most of the world believes. God actually brings the humble up to His dwelling. Isa. 57:15 states:

> **For thus saith the high and lofty One that inhabiteth eternity, whose name is Holy; I dwell in the high and holy place WITH HIM also that is of a contrite and humble spirit, to revive the spirit of the humble, and to revive the heart of the contrite ones.** (Capitals added for emphasis).

Biblical examples of Pride and Humility

God's Word gives us several examples of what it is to exalt ourselves, and what it is to be humble. When Jesus went into the house of one of the chief Pharisees to eat bread, He noticed how those who were bidden chose the chief rooms to sit in. He then said unto them:

> **When thou art bidden of any man to a wedding; sit not down in the highest room; lest a more honourable man than thou be bidden of him; And he that bade thee and him come and say unto thee, Give this man place; and thou begin with shame to take the lowest room. But when thou art bidden, go and sit down in the lowest room; that when he that bade thee cometh, he may say unto thee, Friend, go up higher: then shalt thou have worship in the presence of them that sit at meat with thee** (Lk. 14:7-11).

To choose to sit in the highest rooms is to exalt oneself, but to choose the lowest rooms is an act of humility. This could easily point to the marriage supper of the Lamb where God will exalt those who have lived in humility.

Jesus also spoke about the scribes and Pharisees who did their works to be seen of men. They loved and chose the highest rooms at feasts, and the best seats in the synagogues. They also loved to be called Rabbi of men, and to be greeted in the market places. The term Rabbi literally means 'my great one' or 'my master'. It was not until later that the word became used in reference to an ordinary teacher. Anyway, Jesus informed His disciples that it was not to be this way among them, but he that would be the greatest among them would be their servant (Matt. 23:5-12). This means that those who are the greatest in God's kingdom will be those who humble themselves as servants.

Jesus also told a parable about two men that went into the temple to pray. One was a Pharisee and the other was a publican. The Pharisee stood and prayed:

> **God, I thank thee, that I am not as other men are, extortioners, unjust, adulterers, or even this publican. I fast twice a week, I give tithes of all that I possess. The publican stood afar off, and would not even lift his eyes up to heaven. He smote upon his breast, saying, God be merciful to me a sinner.**

Jesus then said that the publican went to his house justified, not the Pharisee (Lk. 18:9-14). The Pharisee had unwittingly exalted himself, but the publican had humbled himself.

At the Feet of Jesus

We will also find that true humility is to worship at the feet of Jesus. When Jairus, a RULER of the synagogue, came to Jesus he fell at His feet, and then besought Him for the healing of his daughter. As a result, Jesus went with him (Mk. 5:22-24). This reveals that God goes with those of a humble spirit. We need Him to walk with us just as much as we need to walk with Him.

The woman of Canaan that came to Jesus and asked Him to cast a devil out of her daughter also fell at His feet. She stayed humble when Jesus did not answer her at first, and then told her that He was only sent to the lost sheep of the house of Israel. She then worshipped Him, asking for His help. He then said, **"It is not meet to take the children's bread, and cast it to dogs."** The children were those of Israel, the dogs were in reference to the Gentiles. She still responded in humility and faith by saying, **"Truth, Lord: yet the dogs eat of the crumbs which fall from their masters' table."** With everything against her, she still received what she came for (Matt.15:21-28). Humility will cause us to receive from God the things that pride turns away.

A woman named Mary also gives us an excellent example of what it is to be humble. She had a sister named Martha who received Jesus into her house. Martha was cumbered (weighted down) about with much serving, but Mary sat at Jesus' feet and heard His Word. When Martha complained about it, Jesus told her, **"Martha, Martha, thou art careful and troubled about many things: But one thing is needful: and Mary hath chosen that good part, which shall not be taken away from her"** (Lk. 10:38-42).

To be at His feet puts Him first, and puts us in a position to receive from Him. We can still fall at His feet today as we humble ourselves before Him in prayer. One might kneel or just fall with His face to the ground before the Omnipresent God.

Mary is also the woman who washed His feet with her tears, wiped them with her hair, and anointed His feet with an alabaster box of ointment. Others found fault, as she was known to be a woman that had previously lived in sin. Jesus commended her for this great act of love and humility. He stated that she loved much because she had been forgiven for much. He also commended her for her faith. Remember, God resists the proud, but gives grace unto the humble. Faith, which works by love (Gal. 5:6), is an active part of God's grace. As no person deserves anything from God, all is given to us by His grace which, abounds in the life of the humble.

As always, Jesus is our prime example to follow. He is our Lord and Master, but came as a servant. Concerning Him, Phil. 2:5-11 states:

> **Let this mind be in you, which was also in Christ Jesus: Who, being in the form of God, thought it not robbery to be equal with God: But made himself of no reputation, and took upon him the form of a servant, and was made in the likeness of men: And being found in fashion as a man, he humbled himself, and became obedient unto death, even the death of the cross. Wherefore God also hath highly exalted him, and given him a name which is above every name: That at the name of Jesus every knee should bow, of things in heaven, and things in earth, and things under the earth; And that every tongue should confess that Jesus Christ is Lord, to the glory of God the Father.**

Just as God exalted Jesus Christ for His humility, He will also exalt all those that humble themselves in like manner. The more we humble ourselves, the higher God will exalt us.

Chapter 35

THE DOUBLE MINDED

The term 'double minded' is translated from the Greek word 'dipsukos'. It literally means to be double souled. To be double minded is to be divided in ones thinking, to waver or falter between two opinions. It can also speak of one who is double tongued or not truthful. It is a serious matter in the life of a believer. A double minded person has no real ability to believe God's Word as every turn or change of events changes the way he thinks and reacts. A double-minded person is unstable in his Christian walk, and cannot live by faith. James 1:5-8 states:

> **If any of you lack wisdom, let him ask of God, that giveth to all men liberally, and upbraideth not; and it shall be given him. But let him ask in faith, nothing wavering. For he that wavereth is like a wave of the sea driven by the wind and tossed. For let not that man think that he shall receive any thing of the Lord. A double minded man is unstable in all his ways.**

The book of James also gives us other examples of what it is to be double minded. Chapter four begins by speaking of the conflicts that take place among Christians due to the lusts that war in the members of our bodies, and the extremes that some will go to as a means to obtain that which they lust after. We learn that these do not receive or obtain, because they do not ask God, or because they ask amiss to consume it upon their lusts. James speaks of these as committing adultery against God because of their friendship with the world, which puts them at enmity (enemies) with God. It also tells us that God resists them because of their pride (Jas. 4:1-6). Verses 7-8 then states:

> **Submit yourselves therefore unto God. Resist the devil, and he will flee from you. Draw nigh to God, and he will draw nigh to you. Cleanse your hands, ye sinners; and purify your hearts, ye double minded**.

What is spoken of here is an excellent example of a double minded person. He often walks according to the lusts of the flesh rather than after the Spirit. His desires are for earthly things. If he does ask God, he asks for things that are not according to God's will (1 Jn. 5: 14-15). The book of Romans speaks of him as being carnal, one who minds (receives his thoughts) the things of the flesh rather than the things of the Spirit. He continues to love and walk after the course of this world, and refuses to submit himself unto God because of pride (Eph. 2:2, 1 Jn. 2:15).

As we can see from the book of James, this has always been a problem in the church. It was also a problem in the nation of Israel, which gives us very good examples of the things we should be aware of. Idolatry was a big problem in the nation of Israel because of their double mindedness. In the well-known story of Elijah standing against the prophets of Baal on Mount Carmel, he said unto the people, "**How long halt ye between two opinions? if the LORD be God, follow him: but if Baal, then follow him**" (1 Ki. 18:21).

Many believers today also halt between two opinions. They cannot decide whether to serve God fully, or hold on to the things of the world. If we truly believe that Jesus Christ is Lord, it should not be a hard decision.

Israel committed adultery against God, when they worshipped other gods, because they were betrothed to God. Those of the church are betrothed to Christ. We commit adultery against Him when we love and befriend the world. After all, scripture states that Satan is the god of this world (2 Cor. 4:4). Jesus stated:

> **No man can serve two masters: for either he will hate the one, and love the other; or else he will hold to the one, and despise the other. Ye cannot serve God and mammon. Therefore I say unto you, Take no thought for your life, what ye shall eat, or what ye shall drink; nor yet for your body, what ye shall put on. Is not life more that meat, and the body than raiment?** (Matt. 6:24-25).

To take thought of these things is to serve another master. All the things needed for this life are promised to those who seek God's kingdom first, and His righteousness (Matt. 6:33).

To be double minded is also to have a divided heart. Hosea 10:2 states, **"Their heart is divided; now shall they be found faulty: he shall break down their altars, he shall spoil their images"**. Believers should have singleness of heart and mind. We should believe and walk according to God's Word regardless of the way things appear according to the world (or flesh). A divided heart will always doubt and never truly seek God (Mk. 11: 23-24, Deut. 4:29). God's Word praised the fifty thousand of the tribe of Zebulun as they were expert in war and could keep rank, for they were not of a double heart.

Chapter 36

THE SERIOUSNESS OF SEXUAL SIN

What is known as casual sex has become an acceptable lifestyle throughout much of the world. One can hardly watch a movie or a television program that does not have some kind of sexual content. Sexual intercourse is a common practice during dating, casual relationships, and even one night flings. These acts are not looked upon as serious, but just a way to have a good pleasurable experience. Sexual intercourse is never acceptable in God's eyes apart from marriage. It has never been an acceptable lifestyle, nor will it ever be. God's Word makes it very clear that those who commit adultery, fornication, or are effeminate (homosexual) shall not inherit the kingdom of God (1 Cor. 6:9-10).

Sadly to say, sexual immorality has also became more and more accepted and tolerated in much of the church. Many Christians do not even consider it to be a serious sinful act. It has become a very common sin in the church, even among the church leaders. How many pastors have we seen fall because of it? We all know that it is sin, but since so many are involved in it, we have come to believe that it really can't be that bad.

Sexual sin has always been a serious problem for God's people. For examples, King David committed adultery with Bathsheba and then had her husband killed in an attempt to cover it up. Solomon multiplied wives to himself in disobedience to God's Word (Deut. 17:17). Many of his wives were from the nations that God commanded Israel not to marry into. These strange women turned his heart away from following the Lord (1 Ki. 11:1-9).

Almost everyone has strong sexual desires. This is the way God created us to procreate, find pleasure, and enjoy one's mate. However, God has also given us strict guidelines to follow so we will not get these needs met in an ungodly fashion. According to the bible, a sexual relationship is only acceptable in the bonds of marriage. Hebrews 13:4 states, **"Marriage is honourable in all, and the bed undefiled: but whoremongers and adulterers God will judge."** Sexual intercourse apart from marriage defiles those involved.

The Sin of Fornication

To have sexual intercourse outside the bonds of marriage is to commit fornication. Under the Old Covenant, those who were caught committing fornication were commanded to marry. This is because sexual intercourse joins a man and woman together, and the two become one flesh (Gen. 2:24, Mal. 2: 14-16, 1 Cor. 6:16). If a woman was found not to be a virgin on her wedding night, the punishment was to be stoned at the door of her father's house where she had played the whore in Israel (Deut. 22:20-21). The New Testament tells us that we are not to even let fornication be named among us as saints (Eph. 5:3). We have fallen far short of that. We are to be a sanctified (set apart) people. 1 Thess. 4:3-4 states:

> **For this is the will of God, even your sanctification, that ye should abstain from fornication: That everyone of you should know how to possess his vessel in sanctification and honour.**

Those who commit fornication do not sanctify their bodies to the Lord. 1 Cor. 6:13b-18 states:

> **Now the body is not for fornication, but for the Lord, and the Lord for the body. And God hath both raised up the Lord, and will also raise up us by his own power. Know ye not that your bodies are the members of Christ? shall I then take the members of Christ, and make them the members of an harlot? God forbid. What? know ye not that he which is joined to an harlot is one body? for two, saith he, shall be one flesh. But he that is joined to the Lord is one spirit.**

Fornication is spoken of as the only sin that is against one's own body. This is because all other sins are committed outside the body, but fornication is within. We are therefore to flee from it as children of God (1 Cor. 6:18).

The Sin of Adultery

Adultery is committed when a married person has sexual intercourse with any other person other than the one they are married to. Adultery was punishable by death under the Old Covenant as it was to break a blood covenant with one's spouse. A marriage covenant points to our relationship with God. God is spoken of as Israel's husband (Isa. 54:5), and the church is spoken of as the bride of Christ (Eph. 5:22-33). As a man and woman become one flesh by sharing their bodies through sexual intercourse, those who are joined to the Lord through salvation are one spirit (1 Cor. 6:17). They become members of His body, of His flesh, and of His bones (Eph. 5:30).

God's people need to once again realize the sinfulness of sexual immorality. The book of Romans tells us that by the law came the knowledge of sin (Rom. 3:20), and made sin to become exceeding sinful (Rom. 7:13). Sexual sin is so serious that there are entire chapters devoted primarily to it in the Old Testament scriptures (Lev. 18 & 20). The New Testament scriptures also continually warn against it. In almost every list of sins given in the New Testament, adultery and fornication are at the top of the list (Gal. 5:19-21, Eph. 5:3-5, Col. 3:5-6). This is because sexual sin is the most common as a result of the sexual desires that each of us experience.

The Sin of Homosexuality

Homosexuality is another form of sexual immorality that has become more and more accepted throughout much of the world. It is often spoken of as just another acceptable lifestyle. God's Word disagrees. Lev. 18:22 states:

> **Thou shalt not lie with mankind, as with womankind: it is abomination."** Leviticus 20:13 also states, "**If a man also lie with mankind, as he lieth with a woman, both of them have committed an abomination: they shall surely be put to death; their blood shall be upon them.**

This too has also become more accepted and even tolerated in much of the church. There are so called churches today with homosexual pastors, or that have homosexual members of their congregation. There are some that are entirely homosexual. Many seem to be under the false impression that it is acceptable under the New Covenant, which is established on grace, and God will accept them in a homosexual lifestyle. That is not what the Bible teaches. Romans 1:26-27 states:

> **For this cause God gave them up unto vile affections: for even their women did change the natural use into that which is against nature: And likewise also the men, leaving the natural use of the woman, burned in lust one toward another; men with men working that which is unseemly, and receiving in themselves that recompence of their error which was meet.**

Homosexuality is an erroneous lifestyle that is against nature, or the natural way that God created things to be. The bible calls it a vile affection for any person to lust after one of the same sex. Those who live this lifestyle will receive in themselves the recompense of their error, and are prone to deadly sexually transmitted diseases such as AIDS. Those who live this lifestyle will experience the wrath of God. The destruction of the cities of Sodom and Gomorrah is set forth as an example for those who would later live this ungodly lifestyle (2 Pet. 2:6).

A child of God needs to bring their lives into obedience to God's Word concerning this subject. If one cannot abstain, to avoid fornication, every man is to have his own wife, and every woman is to have her own husband. They are not to defraud each other, or be with another. They are to satisfy each other's desires and needs (1 Cor. 7:1-5). This is the natural order of the way God created it to be.

Chapter 37

GOD'S ENABLING GRACE

We often hear about God's grace in reference to our salvation, but little about how it affected our lives before we were saved, or how it continues to work in our lives afterward. A good and simple definition for grace is God's unmerited favor. This is because there is nothing we can do to earn or deserve anything from God because of our sinful nature. Everything we receive from God is a gift of His grace.

God's Manifold Grace

The greatest gift of God's grace is His Son Jesus Christ. Even though we deserved nothing from Him, He still gave us His Son as a means of salvation to all that believe in Him. As a result, God's grace is in Jesus Christ (2 Tim. 2:1). As God delivered Him up for us all, He now freely gives us all things with Him (Rom. 8:32). God's Word states, **"And of his fulness have all we received, and grace for grace. For the law was given by Moses, but grace and truth came by Jesus Christ"** (Jn. 1:16-17). When the Word speaks here of grace for grace, it means we continue to receive one grace after another. God's grace is manifold (1 Pet. 4:10). To be manifold means to be many sided, to have multiple layers, and to be various in character.

We receive far more from God's grace than just salvation. We were elected by grace (Rom. 11:5), called to salvation by grace (Gal. 1:6, 15), believe through grace (Acts 18:27), and were saved by grace (Eph. 2:5, 8). After salvation, God works through grace to bring forth holiness, growth and services. Titus 2:11-14 states:

> **For the grace of God that bringeth salvation hath appeared to all men, teaching us that, denying ungodliness and worldly lusts, we should live soberly, righteously, and godly, in this present world; Looking for that blessed hope, and the glorious appearing of the great God and Saviour Jesus Christ; Who gave himself for us, that he might redeem us from all iniquity, and purify unto himself a peculiar people, zealous of good works.**

This leaves us without excuse for willful sin or neglect of our Christian services. God empowers us through grace to keep His Word, to live as we should, and to be able to accomplish whatever He has called us to do.

Grace Enables us to Walk in Our Calling

To receive grace means that God is doing something in a person's life. It is by grace that we receive spiritual enlightenment from His Word, faith, deliverances, or any other spiritual blessing that brings growth in our lives. God's Word states that He has before ordained us to good works (Eph. 2:10). God has equipped each of us by His grace to walk in the good works we are ordained to. For a good example let's look at the Apostle Paul. Paul stated that he was an apostle of Jesus Christ by the commandment of God (1 Tim. 1:1). He therefore had no choice or say in the matter. However God did equip him for this service by His grace. Paul stated:

> **But by the grace of God I am what I am: and his grace which was bestowed upon me was not in vain; but I**

> **laboured more abundantly than them all: yet not I, but the grace of God which was with me** (1 Cor. 15:10).

Paul labored more abundantly than all the other apostles, speaking of those who actually walked with the Lord Jesus. Yet he recognized that it was not actually himself, but a work of God's grace.

God's Word tells us that we are workers together with God, and beseeches us not to receive the grace of God in vain (2 Cor. 6:1). So we can receive God's grace in vain. Those who do not mature in their Christian walk, or do not walk in their calling do so. Paul often spoke of the measure of grace that was given to him, and that which he accomplished, or was gifted with as a result. The Word states that the apostles that had walked with the Lord had great grace (Acts 4:33). This enabled them to give witness to the resurrection of the Lord with great power. They are examples of not receiving God's grace in vain.

The Depths of God's Grace

Individuals, who were deep in sin before salvation, should never think or feel that they cannot or will not be used by God. The Word states that where sin abounded, grace did much more abound. It takes a great amount of grace to save those who were deep in sin (Rom. 6:20). That same measure of grace remains in their lives after salvation. That means they have great potential by that grace to be mightily used by God. Once again, Paul is an excellent example. He stated:

> **And I thank Jesus Christ our Lord, who hath enabled me, for that he counted me faithful, putting me in the ministry; Who was before a blasphemer, and a persecutor, and injurious: but I obtained mercy, because I did it ignorantly in unbelief. And the grace of our Lord was exceeding abundant with faith and love which is in Christ Jesus. This is a faithful saying, and worthy of all acceptation, that Christ Jesus came**

into the world to save sinners; of whom I am chief (1 Tim. 1:12-15).

The apostle Paul was the chief of sinners before salvation, and the greatest used apostle after salvation. All God's children have great potential through God's manifold grace. There is no limit to what God will do in the lives of those who continue to grow in grace (2 Pet. 3:18).

Chapter 38

AN EXPECTED END

"For I know the thoughts that I think toward you, saith the LORD, thoughts of peace, and not of evil, to give you an expected end" (Jeremiah 29:11).

The expected end that is spoken of in this passage of scripture is in reference to the end we hope for, the end that God has promised us, and on which He has caused us to hope. God's Word tells us to mark the perfect man, and behold the upright: for the end of that man is peace (Ps. 37:37).

It is very comforting to know that God is always at work in the life of every believer. Phil. 1:6 states, **"Being confident of this very thing, that he which hath begun a good work in you will perform it until the day of Jesus Christ."** God begins a good work in the life of every believer upon salvation. It is not a work that He will ever stop or leave undone. He will continue that work until bringing it to completion on the day of Jesus Christ. Eccl. 7:8 states, **"Better is the end of a thing than the beginning thereof."** God never begins anything that He does not finish and bring to an end. He tells us in His Word, **"when I begin, I will also make an end"** (1 Sam. 3:12b). He also tells us through Jacob:

> **And, behold, I am with thee, and will keep thee in all places whither thou goest, and will bring thee again into this land; for I will not leave thee, until I have done that which I have spoken to thee of** (Gen. 28:15).

God will leave none of His children until He has done everything that He has spoken in His Word concerning us.

There is much work that God must do in each of our lives to bring us to the end that He has promised us. The life of a child of God is not always easy, but the things we must go through or endure are not worthy to be compared to the end result of what God is doing in our lives (Rom 8:18). There are many things in each of our lives that God must cleanse, purge, and deliver us from. This means that we may go through some hard and trying times as God cleanses and purges our lives. We may go through and experience things that we do not always understand, or even see God's purpose behind them. At times it can seem like God has left and forsaken us, but this is never the case. The times that we think that God is the farthest from us, and is doing the least in our lives because of what we might be going through, are the times when He is the closest and doing the greatest works.

Forty Years in the Wilderness

Let's look at some examples in God's Word. After God delivered the nation of Israel out of Egypt, they then wondered in the wilderness for the next forty years before entering into their promised land; which was only an eleven day journey from mount Horeb (Deut. 1:2). The book of Ezekiel informs us that the people of Israel did not cast away and forsake the gods of Egypt, and they rebelled against God in the wilderness, as they did not walk in His statutes and judgments (Ezekiel chapter 20). If that first generation had entered into their promised land they would have carried Egypt (a type of the world) right into the land with them. God purged Egypt out of them as they wandered in the wilderness for those forty years.

Israel went through some trying times in the wilderness. Many of their journeys were hard and the soul of the people would get discouraged because of the way (Num. 21:4). There were times of hunger and thirst. Much of the time they did not know where their next meal or drink would come from. They often felt as if it would have been better for them to have stayed in Egypt, as they were not in possession of the land that God had promised them at that time. God had a reason for all of this. Speaking to the second generation that went in and possessed the land, Deut. 8:1-3 states:

> **All the commandments which I command thee this day shall ye observe to do, that ye may live, and multiply, and go in and possess the land which the LORD sware unto your fathers. And thou shalt remember all the way which the LORD thy God led thee these forty years in the wilderness, to humble thee, and to prove thee, to know what was in thine heart, whether thou wouldest keep his commandments, or no. And he humbled thee, and suffered thee to hunger, and fed thee with manna, which thou knewest not, neither did thy fathers know; that he might make thee know that man doth not live by bread only, but by every word that proceedeth out of the mouth of the LORD doth man live.**

God needed to humble and prove (test) them to reveal what was really in their hearts, and to know whether or not they would keep His commandments. The main reason a person needs to be humbled is because of pride. A prideful person lives for himself, does not like to be told what to do, and will therefore not keep God's commandments. Of course God already knew what was in their hearts, but it had to be brought out through the afflictions, trials, and temptations they experienced.

God then told them to consider in their hearts, that, as a man chasteneth his son, so the Lord thy God chastened them (Deut. 8:5). Chastening is for the purpose of bringing correction. He needed to correct them so that they would keep His commandments, walk in His way, and fear Him before He brought them into the land of their inheritance (Deut. 8:6-7).

He also told them to beware and not forget the things they went through in the wilderness, and turn away from Him, when they would be living in abundance in the land He was giving them. Deut. 8:15-16, then states:

> **Who led thee through that great and terrible wilderness, wherein were fiery serpents, and scorpions, and drought, where there was no water; who brought thee forth water out of the rock of flint; Who fed thee in the wilderness with manna, which thy fathers knew not, that he might humble thee, and that he might prove thee, TO DO THEE GOOD AT THY LATTER END** (Capitals added for emphasis).

There was a purpose for everything they went through in the wilderness. God's main concern is to do us good, not evil, at our latter end.

How It Applies to Our Lives

Israel wandering in the wilderness for forty years, until the first generation died off, is a type of us living in this world after salvation. At salvation we are not ready to receive the fullness of our inheritance. This is where God cleanses, purges, and delivers us from the things of this world. This is where we put off (put to death) the old man from our first birth, and put on the new man from our second birth, that will cross over into the fullness of our inheritance.

As we wonder as strangers and pilgrims in this world after salvation, we will also go through similar experiences to that of Israel during their wilderness wandering. None of us are really any different. Those of the church also refuse to cast away and forsake many of the things of this world, which is idolatry. It is obvious as we look at the condition of much of the church that we are not walking in obedience to God's Word. Pride is one of many things that are in every believer's life to some degree.

We must also go through similar things for God to humble and prove us, to know what is in our hearts, and to work the world out of us. We will experience God's chastisement to bring correction to our lives, which causes us to rely on Him, and to bring our lives into obedience to His Word. God's Word says that God chastens those whom He loves, and scourges every son He receives. Every one of His children is a partaker of his chastisement. God's chastisement is for our profit that we might be partakers of his holiness. It seems grievous as we endure it, but it afterwards yields the peaceable fruit of righteousness unto them which are exercised thereby (Heb. 12:5-11).

There are times when our lives can get very difficult and our souls get discouraged because of our Christian walk. There can be times when God suffers us to hunger or thirst (naturally or spiritually) due to the loss of a job, finances, or other worldly possessions to see if we will keep His Word and trust in Him through the experience, or not. There can be those times when we feel like it was better for us before we ever came unto salvation, and are tempted to go back to the world. There will be times when it does not seem as though we possess anything that God has promised us.

All of these things are only for a season and will pass. We must go through all of these things because God wants the very best for us. He instructs us to remember when He humbles and proves us, that our hearts will never get lifted up, and we forget Him and His work of salvation; for after we endure we receive His abundant blessings (Deut. 8:7-14).

Job's Expected End

Another great example is Job. Scripture actually introduces us to Job as being perfect and upright, and a man that feared God and shunned evil (Job 1:1). Job appeared to have everything. He had a wife and ten children. He was also a great man of wealth and influence. However, under God's supervision and according to His sovereign plan, Job came under an attack from Satan and lost practically everything he had. He lost all his possessions, his children, and even the respect and influence he once had in his community; all in one day. The events that took place in Job's life are very confusing to many who wonder why God would permit Job to go through such terrible things. After all, God never makes any direct reference to sin in Job's life.

As we live this life there is always room for improvement. Remember, God is working to bring us to that expected end. As we study the book of Job, we do find areas of his life that needed some improvement. For one thing, Job had fear in his life. Job stated in the first dialogue with his friends:

> **For the thing which I greatly feared is come upon me, and that which I was afraid of is come unto me. I was not in safety, neither had I rest, neither was I quiet; yet trouble came"** (Job 3:25-26).

Job was not a man living with inner peace. The tragic events that took place in Job's life were all things that he feared. This shows that his love was not perfect, which also would have affected his faith. 1 John 4:18 states, **"There is no fear in love; but perfect love casteth out fear: because fear hath torment. He that feareth is not made perfect in love."** As faith works by love (Gal. 5:6), his faith was not nearly as strong as it could have been.

For another thing, Job appears to have been a very self-righteous man. He uses the words I, my, and me fifty times in the twenty-five verses of chapter twenty-nine. In this chapter he attributed his righteousness, wealth, works, and high standing to himself; and gave God little to no credit at all (see Job chapter 29). His three friends eventually ceased to answer Job because he was righteous in his own eyes (Job 32:1).

God used these afflictions to do a great work to try and prove Job's life. In the end he was no longer living in fear, but had a greater love for God. His faith also had been tried and purified (1 Pet. 1:6-7). He was no longer self-righteous, but humble before the Lord. Job 42:12-13 states:

> **So the LORD blessed the latter end of Job more than his beginning: for he had fourteen thousand sheep, and six thousand camels, and a thousand yoke of oxen, and a thousand she asses. He had also seven sons and three daughters.**

Comparing this to what Job had before his affliction, God gave him double of what he had before. He then lived an hundred and forty years after all this and saw his grandsons to the fourth generation (Job 42:16). In reference to this, James 5:11, states, **"Behold, we count them happy which endure. Ye have heard of the patience of Job, AND SEEN THE END OF THE LORD; that the Lord is very pitiful, and of tender mercy"** (Capitals added for emphasis).

God surely uses these same methods in our lives today. No matter what it might be that we go through (or are going through), God is in control and will see us through it. There will be an end, and God will have done something great and wonderful in our lives. Proverbs 27:18 states, **"For surely there is an end; and thine expectation shall not be cut off."**

ABOUT THE AUTHOR

Dale Heil, the author of this book, spent several years in the Colorado prison system. A few months into his incarceration he received the Lord Jesus Christ, and dedicated his life to the service of the Lord. He has a love for God's Word, and dedicated most of his time to the study of it. After a period of time, the prison bible studies were not enough to satisfy his hunger for God's Word, and his strong desire to know more. He then began to pray for deeper insight in the Word, and God revealed it to him. He eventually began to teach bible studies to other inmates, and did so until his release. He and another inmate started a ministry, from the inside, called Spirit and Life, which seemed to be a fitting title to this book. These bible studies has continued to have a profound effect on God's people inside and outside of prison walls.

www.ingramcontent.com/pod-product-compliance
Lightning Source LLC
LaVergne TN
LVHW041800060526
838201LV00046B/1072